AWAKENING
the
SOUL

*A Deep Response
to a Troubled World*

AWAKENING
the
SOUL

*A Deep Response
to a Troubled World*

MICHAEL MEADE

GREENFIRE PRESS
An Imprint of Mosaic Multicultural Foundation

GREENFIRE PRESS
An Imprint of Mosaic Multicultural Foundation

Cover Illustration

The Monk by the Sea, by Casper David Friedrich, painted over a two year period beginning in 1808.

CONTENTS

Introduction 3

Part I: Waking the Underlying Soul

1 The World Weary Man 15

2 Indelible Marks of the Soul 29

3 Life on Edge 47

4 Inner Eyes of Soul 59

5 The Prison We Are In 75

Part II: The Search for Meaning and Truth

6 Getting to the Bottom of Things 91

7 The Forgotten Story 106

8 The Soul's Great Adventure 123

9 Turning Things Around 138

10 The Bird of Truth 156

The individual soul is a microcosm, a realm in itself.
If penetrated deeply, it turns inside-out
and becomes the Soul of the World.

INTRODUCTION

A WORLD UPSIDE DOWN

·

The great moments in life, whether in the life of an individual or an entire culture, are existential crises—moments that challenge all aspects of society and all levels of human awareness. We have entered such an extended moment of radical change and alteration, one that is life-defining as well as life-changing. When the troubles become worldwide, affecting both nature and culture, it is time to face up to what has been building up for a long time. Because all things are ultimately interconnected, the challenges we face and the changes underway signal a genuine transformation of the world.

There is no way to simply think our way through the troubles that threaten the world, although clarifying issues can help. There is no magic bullet, singular solution, or technological fix. There can be no "work around" when the issues have become too large in scope to ignore or simply slip past. Issues like global warming and climate change have become too big for current institutions to handle, while the complex web of cultural troubles we face are too great for most politicians to fully grasp, much less fix. Despite the political rhetoric, there can be no simple fixes as self-interest and short-term thinking cannot solve worldwide problems or long-term issues.

In some sense, the world has fallen asleep and is suffering a loss of the dream of life, leaving us with nightmares that produce pollution in nature as well as poisons in culture. There is a growing "collective trauma" as the hollowing of institutions and flood of rapid changes can cause everyone to become "dis-oriented" and feel disillusioned by the daily conditions of life. Traumatizing agents include the rise of mass culture and the subsequent diminishing of the individual soul, the spread of rampant materialism, and the rise of "connective" technologies that contribute to deep disconnections while "linking" people at surface levels of life.

In a world gone wrong, any issue can polarize society, divide nations and religions, and push people to the edge of despair. Painful divisions in the realms of culture have been there all along, serious injuries have gone unhealed for decades, and great injustices have been routinely ignored. Now, all the underlying angers, resentments, and fears have been stirred up and have risen to the surface. Just as deep toxins are released when an old wound is opened up or ruptures, we are experiencing a return of all the repressed fears and feelings.

We have wandered far from the origins of life and from the essential originality of the soul's knowing center. We have become cosmologically dislocated and caught in the backspin of time and the turmoil of a world turning upside down.

We live in a time of overwhelming challenges and seemingly impossible tasks. Yet, this is not the end of time, but a break in the rhythm of history that also creates openings to the realm of great imagination and the possibility of reconnecting to the Soul of the World. When time cracks, the moment opens to eternity, making knowledge and wisdom available. Such moments of awakening become "lived time;" time fully lived in which we awaken to a greater sense of the world and our place in it.

Change is the essence of life; but as people face great changes and an unknown future, they tend to become fearful. As fear spreads, most try to cling to something familiar and try to control things in order to reduce the terror of being overwhelmed. Yet, the overwhelming lesson of history, on both collective and individual levels, is that closing down and holding tight to familiar things does not work. Amid such massive disorientation one of the few ways to find sense and meaning is to find the inner order, the shape and style of one's own soul. No matter what threats and disasters occur at the surface of life, the underlying soul remains an endless resource and vital source of change and renewal.

When life becomes severely polarized, when people become more opposed than they need to be, it is the connective energy and unifying presence of soul that has gone missing. Meaningful solutions to deeply penetrating and broad-reaching problems require the kind of imaginative vision and innovative invention that can only be found in the depths of the human soul. If there is no change at the level of soul, there can be no meaningful change at the level of the world. After all, the human soul has an innate connection to nature and an intrinsic concern for the entire planet as well as the cosmos.

The modern world, plagued by false rhetoric and tormented by intensifying polarities and ancient animosities, suffers from a collective loss of soul. Given the size and dimensions of contemporary problems and the fact that all aspects of both culture and nature are threatened, this is the exact time to awaken the underlying soul that secretly sustains both individual life and the life of the earth. What we are facing is not simply a collapse of culture or a clash of civilizations; rather we are in a struggle for the dignity and meaning of the individual soul and a battle for the Soul of the World.

ABOUT THIS BOOK

This is a book about the necessity of soul at a time when the world seems to be losing its soul. This is a book about the human soul; but also about the underlying Soul of the World. It is about the necessity of waking the deep resources of the soul and making more soul at a time of widespread divisions and growing disasters. This is a book about the awakening of the individual soul and the capacity of each soul to contribute to the healing and renewal of a world gone wrong.

Soul is the glue of the world and the connecting principle of life; as such, it is the missing component when everything has fallen apart. When the whole world turns upside down, it is the soul at the bottom of everything that is trying to become known again. Soul connects us to things that are deep and abiding in the world and in our own lives. The depths of soul contain the vitality of life, the core powers of imagination, and the ancient inheritance of humanity.

Loss of soul leads to the feeling that life lacks meaning; that being alive on earth has no real purpose. This is a book about living with meaning at a time when many people doubt that there is any meaning in the world at all. Soul adds a felt-sense of psychic reality to common experiences; it is the deep presence of the individual soul that makes life meaningful. When we see with the eyes of the soul, every event—inner or outer—can be seen to have meaning.

Truth and meaning are essential needs of the human soul that often go missing in the modern world, in which cleverness and cunning try to substitute for genuine meaning and purpose. We find ourselves in a time of radical change when the world, with its many levels of experience and many varieties of truth, must shift from one level to another. When the world goes upside down, those things that are most important in life can slip from our grip and seemingly fall out of reach. Then, it is time to go looking for essential things that are missing in the depths of the soul.

This is a book about the need to touch and claim ancient ideas and imaginings in order to survive modern dilemmas and become able to aid in the renewal of the world. We need radical ideas and transcendent imaginings, the kind that can only be found in the depths of the soul of humanity.

The counterbalance to the increasing chaos in daily life must be found in the depths of individual souls awakening to the inborn sense of meaning and purpose in life. An old idea states that nature only makes originals. Each tree that stands, each flower that blooms, and each soul born must be unique in some way. Each soul, regardless of outer circumstances or appearances, is born with an inner nobility and sense of purpose that longs to become known and be given a chance to manifest. Denying an individual or a group of people the opportunity to find and follow their life dreams is not simply a mistake; it is also an assault on their natural nobility and an insult to the soul.

This is a book about the awakening and initiation of both the individual soul and the collective soul of culture. The soul would have us become who and what we are in our essence, at our core before we are even born. When a person—regardless of their age, education, or background—acts from the depths of their soul, they add imagination and unique presence as well as meaning and beauty to the world. Each soul carries within it the "force of truth." When enough people awaken to the inherent purpose and meaning in their own lives, a collective initiation can also occur and shift the level of meaning and the course of history.

Soul is the invisible center of life, the middle term of all things, and the glue that connects culture to nature. Soul is what gives movement to life and soul is what holds things together in a secret continuity of being. This is the saving grace in life, a paradox in which soul is both the source of the hidden unity of the world and the vital force of diversity and multiplicity in both nature and culture. Soul is the blessed intimacy of all things. The thread of our inner nature invisibly connects us to the mysteries of the cosmos as well as the heart of Nature.

This book is about the necessity of awakening to the underlying story of the soul, the inner pattern and living plotline for the life that we have chosen, but have also forgotten. In one sense, we are each born with an original soul; in another, we must make more soul in order to truly become ourselves. Only then can we deliver to the world—so often ruled by disparity, fear, and uncertainty—the hidden abundance of the soul.

The soul underlies all great projects, including the life adventure of each soul born. This is a book about the underlying soul trying to awaken within us—trying to wake us up to the dream that carried us to the threshold between worlds and the birth of our unique adventure on earth. This is a book about the necessity of finding more soul in our lives and about making more soul in the world.

This is a book about inner meanings, about finding purpose when all seems pointless. Yet, it is not about being simply heroic or blindly willful. The mind may wish to get straight to the point; but the soul prefers to go off the beaten track and circle around to arrive at important things. In following soul, this book shifts between mythic tales, personal stories and ancient ideas in order to find crucial points of meaning and revelation.

Awakening the Soul begins with a description of one of the oldest stories ever found. On a papyrus scroll written 4500 years ago, an Egyptian scribe laments the condition of his culture, which includes violence, loss of all civility and the collapse of major institutions. Despite the age of the manuscript, the author could be describing the conditions of our contemporary world, which also suffers from the withering effects of collective anxiety and the isolating results of a collective loss of soul.

Subsequent chapters draw upon ancient ideas and stories that describe the importance of finding and making more soul as an antidote to the pressures and problems occurring at a collective level. As the deepest power of the human soul, imagination is shown to be a crucial element in finding creative solutions to otherwise overwhelming problems. Ancient ideas and practices of initiation deepen the understanding of ways in which individuals truly transform and learn to affect greater change at a cultural level.

Awakening the Soul, presents the idea of "living in truth" as an individual way to respond to the use of big lies, campaigns of false information, and the idea of a "post-truth" world. Although we are facing a global environmental crisis and a worldwide humanitarian crisis involving social injustice, there is a third crisis that deeply affects the other two. This third level of peril involves a "crisis of meaning" exemplified by the loss of truth and meaning currently affecting leadership and politics worldwide. Without the pursuit of meaning and truth, there can be no enduring solutions for the crises that threaten nature and human culture.

Despite the growing confusions and distractions of the modern world, we are the current inheritors of the deep human longings for truth and beauty and the life-sustaining capacity to transform. Transformation at the level of the individual soul generates the imagination and collective energy needed to change the conditions of the world. What we need is not a minor repair, but a major transformation of the world that can only start from the inside. The true path for changing and healing the world lies in the awakening of the individual soul.

I

WAKING *the* UNDERLYING SOUL

CHAPTER 1

THE WORLD WEARY MAN

Whoever would move the world must first move their soul.

As people of the modern world, we tend to imagine things in terms of history and feel ourselves to be at the front edge of the march of time. If you ask where paper comes from, you will likely learn the history of its making and the latest methods of manufacture. People in the ancient world, by contrast, often felt connected to things that were timeless and aligned with cosmic rhythms. In the ancient world, looking for the origins of paper might lead one all the way back to the beginning, before time and history even began. The prevailing idea was that everything had to have been there from the beginning—even something as thin as a sheet of paper could be traced all the way back to the time of creation and the beginning of life on earth.

The word *paper* comes from the Greek *papyrus*, but the story of it derives from what, in Egyptian myth, was called the "first occasion," or the onset of creation. That occasion, which made all other occasions, subsequent events, and histories possible, began when nothing could be seen except the endless darkness of the primordial ocean called "nun." Nothing could be seen, yet everything was there, hidden and concealed in the darkness.

Then, a mound of earth rose from the none-ness, or nothingness, of nun and that pyramid-shaped hill was the first sign of the world. It was the beginning of the earth and its shape would be repeated in the form of temples and pyramids, some of which still stand on the ancient land. From the mound that had first risen from the dark waters there soon arose the sun, which began to reveal the light that had also been concealed. As the revelations of the first occasion continued, life sprang forth at the edges of the primordial hill, where reeds rose from the unseen depths and dark waters of nothing and nun.

Because the reeds first appeared at the edge formed by the primal waters and original mound of earth, they were considered to be connected to the roots and unseen source of all of creation. As the primal kernels of creation, the seeds of those plants represented the ever-renewable essence of life. When the first people came along, it was these papyrus plants that provided them with the material for making clothes and shelter. The fibers of the reeds were used for food and the stems for making baskets to hold the food. Eventually, the stalks were tied tightly together and shaped into skiffs used to navigate through the marshes and gather great quantities of the primeval plants.

When the time was right for writing to begin, it was the pith of those reeds that was pounded and shaped by hand and turned into sheets. And, when the first forms of paper were rolled into scrolls, a papyrus reed was placed at the center and a piece of papyrus string used to hold it together. It is in that sense that the thread of writing can be seen to be tied all the way back to the beginning of time. Despite the ravages of time and the obliterating sands of history, some of those ancient manuscripts have survived. While some scrolls simply describe tallies of grains and seeds for storage, other manuscripts represent some of the oldest pieces of writing in the history of the world.

A particular remnant of a tattered scroll written on papyrus over 4,500 years ago seems to have survived for a reason. An unnamed author, deeply discouraged by the state of the world in which he lived, finds himself at the edge of despair and on the verge of self-destruction. In one of the oldest stories ever recorded, he depicts a state of growing anxiety and anguish over the collapse of social life. He questions whether living has any meaning, whether life has any genuine purpose in a world gone wrong.

To whom can I speak these days, when hearts have become rapacious and everyone takes their neighbor's goods?
To whom can I speak these days, when brothers turn against brother, when even friends won't offer love?
And, why speak at all when gentleness has perished and violent men openly slay whomever they will?
Why speak when most are intrigued with evil and goodness becomes neglected everywhere?

Although these are not the words of a contemporary person, they could be. Because the name of the ancient writer will never be known; he could be anyone, he could speak for everyone. He could be speaking of conditions prevalent right now instead of thousands of years ago. Because he lived during a turbulent time and felt the weight of the world upon him, he came to be known as the World Weary Man. Because we live in a time of global upheaval and radical change, we can feel a great weight and isolating pressure and feel world weary as well.

The World Weary Man's lament continues with the aching

feelings of being isolated and having no one to speak with when it comes to the deeper issues of life and the distress of human suffering and isolation.

To whom could I speak anyway? No one remembers the wisdom of the past; no one now helps those who struggle for good in the world.
When the truth of suffering all over the world is mentioned, everyone seeks to lay blame on others.
To whom can I speak, when those who would speak for justice have gone silent and the land is left to the doers of harm?
To whom can I turn, when there is no intimate friend, no heart that I can trust and only my own misery endures?
Death is in my sight today and it looks like a clearing in the sky. Put down my misery!

The unknown author painfully states that he has become weary of life and describes the array of troubles that bring him to the edge of existence. Clearly, he has experienced significant personal disappointments in life. Just as clearly, he suffers from the oppression and injustice of the times. He describes a country that is deeply unsettled and people who are suffering from increasing turmoil and an erosion of ethical values. Wide-scale injustice, excessive greed, and the spread of mindless violence have brought him to despair. Wounded by the mendacity of powerful people and the emptiness of his culture, he falls into a dark night of the soul. He considers suicide as a way out of the tragedy and chaos that surround him.

At that point, when all his sympathies have been depleted and he sees nowhere else to turn, he instinctively turns inward. With the weight of the world on his shoulders, at a moment when death seems like a relief from all the burdens of life, he aims his lament at what was known as his life-spirit, or Ba-soul. And, from a place of deeper understanding and greater perspective on life, his soul answers him.

And my soul said to me: My companion and brother, cast aside your complaints, make offerings on the altar and struggle for your life.
Thrust aside this longing for the West; appreciate your life in this world. You will attain the West when your body becomes ready to go to earth, after you are truly world weary; then we shall both go and make an abode in that world together.

The beginning of the manuscript is missing altogether and the writing ends just as abruptly, at a tattered edge of torn papyrus. Where we might hope for a clear decision in favor of life, the tale ends inconclusively. The scroll somehow survives the scorns of time but remains forever incomplete. Century after century, this twist of fate leaves the fortune of the ancient writer hanging in the air, along with his burning questions about the meaning and purpose of life. Yet, there is something appropriate about these questions remaining unanswered, just as the troubles of the world, which grow greater and greater, continue to be unresolved.

The timeworn document makes clear that the sense of hopelessness does not simply develop from the writer's own personal problems. Although his consideration of suicide indicates his personal anguish, there is also a clear expression of cultural angst and collective anxiety. He suffers his fate in a deeply personal way, but the suffering derives in part from deteriorating cultural conditions. The weight of social unrest and collective fear adds to his personal sense of alienation from life.

The ancient writer likely lived in a period after Egypt had reached the height of its power and materialistic culture. The reign of the Old Kingdom had begun to crumble, giving way to a time of anarchy, feuding factions, and ubiquitous violence. Responsible government was collapsing and institutions were crumbling. Even the pyramids were sacked and sacred artifacts belonging to the dead stolen away. This collapse led to an era of extreme disruption, bewilderment, and despair as the stability of the Egyptian world turned upside down.

COLLECTIVE ANXIETY

Like the anguished scribe, we live in tormented and troubling times. The world around us rattles and all of life's conflicts and uncertainties seem to surface at the same time. The anguished condition of the World Weary Man can represent our own state of mind. However, the levels of insecurity and anxiety are more amplified at this time. Collective anxiety and depression were present when writing on papyrus was just beginning; but to be alive now means to experience the pressure of worldwide disruption occurring in both nature and culture at the same time. Along with an increase in general anxiety, global-scale problems such as climate change, cultural extremism, and terrorism leave us with a growing sense of helplessness.

The ancient document makes clear that the loss of meaning and shared values in a culture causes individuals to suffer greatly at a psychological level. It is as if the purpose of its endurance is not simply to record the pain of individual suffering, but also to remind us that what troubles the world must also deeply trouble us as individuals. At issue way back then, as it is again now, was collective anxiety, along with a growing sense of despair and deep uncertainty about the future of the world. Amid profound changes and deepening uncertainties, anxiety becomes a free-floating collective state.

In contrast to the long-departed world—a time when paper was made by hand—we now live in a time when events move faster and faster and news seems to travel at the speed of light. As collective troubles and worldwide dangers grow both in number and scale, news of tragedies and disasters reaches most people instantaneously. The scale of problems and the speed of change in the modern world can leave the heart and the soul of humanity feeling not only left behind, but increasingly powerless as well.

Amidst increasing amounts of polarization and "tribalization" at all levels of social and political life, there is a greater possibility for people to experience "global despair." As once repressed fears and enmities, grandiosities and atrocities appear on the stage of life at the same time, a kind of "global acting out" occurs. Events don't just feel out of one's own control, but beyond anyone's control.

When enough disparity, avarice, and dishonesty grow in a society, the level of despair also begins to swell under the surface of life. When violence, misogyny, and hatred are allowed to fester, there will be an increase of fear and misery in everyone. The individual heart cannot help but feel heavy and increasingly burdened with the collective weight of suffering and the turbulence of cultural upheaval. Yet, it is not simply that the issues in the current world are so great as to overwhelm everyone at times, but also that so many people feel increasingly isolated and alone.

While both ancient and modern people have found themselves facing issues of radical change and cultural alienation, the ancient scribe did not feel completely alone in life, as a person can so easily feel today. Were he alive now, the lamenting scribe might point out that although mass communication at rapid speeds may be available to almost everyone, people frequently have no one to talk to or share their burdens with. Despite all the ways of being connected to the modern world, in the depths of ourselves we feel more isolated and alienated than ever before. Although everything is supposedly at our fingertips, we can find ourselves increasingly out of touch with what we need at the level of our souls. With the loss of soul we lose the understanding that we are all in this together. We lose the sense that each person is wounded by life and therefore naturally deserving of sympathy and respect.

COLLECTIVE LOSS OF SOUL

It is one thing for a culture to become caught in the turmoil of change and uncertainty; that has happened repeatedly throughout the history of the world. It is quite another thing to forget or lose the sense that we have an inner soul that can hold us close to life even in our darkest hours. The great difference between the ancient scribe and the anxious citizen of the modern world may be experienced as a loss of soul. In ancient times, the existence of the human soul was not often in question. Thus, to live at a time when there is a growing loss of soul means to inherit a greater than usual weight of collective depression and existential anxiety.

How strange it seems that something that was documented when documentation was just beginning could now become mostly forgotten. Or, maybe it is not strange at all if we consider that the most common source of alienation and depression is forgetting that which is most important to us. No matter the time in history or the place in the world, the greatest cause of despair comes from not knowing who we truly are. Not who others want us to be or expect us to be; but who and what we truly are at the core of our souls. In the midst of all the anxiety and uncertainty, something subtle yet enduring about humanity and the world is waiting to rise like the original mound of earth and be discovered again.

Most ancient people and traditional cultures imagined some sort of soulful presence that accompanied a person throughout the course of life. Such notions now confound people. A narrow sense of rationality and logic dominates modern life. Many modern people doubt that there is any such thing as a self-defining human soul. Yet, there is and *must* be something essential in each of us— something not simply born of genetics and biology, or bred from some random selection of genes. At the deeper levels of being, each person born must be, in some way, unique. Otherwise, life becomes nothing but duplication, imitation, and blind mutation.

One of the few things that can stand against the vacancy of mass culture and the onslaught of radical change is the sense of an animating inner soul that makes each person uniquely and essentially valuable. As the original agent of our lives and source of our talents and gifts, the human soul stands against the loss of meaning and purpose so characteristic of modern cultures.

Although an elusive concept, soul has traditionally been seen as the underlying substance and distinct force of each person's character and way of being. By virtue of our souls, we are each connected to the essential pulse of life, to the core powers of imagination, and potentially, to the ancient inheritance of humanity. Thus, the soul is both ancient and immediate; it is enduring as well as spontaneous. It is in the depths of the human soul, where mystery resides, that history can be continually remade.

When everything seems to be falling apart, soul is the missing ingredient; but the problem is that the presence of the human soul cannot be proven in logical, scientific terms. We cannot analyze, categorize, or contain it; yet we can tell when it is missing. Those who seek to prove the existence of the soul are simply not meeting the issue at the right level. The soul is part of the deeper, more intuitive levels of human understanding, where simple reasoning must give way to things that are not only irrational, but also numinous and mysterious.

The rational mind reels and falters from all the irrational blows coming from both cultural and natural disasters. A greater psychological awareness is required and a deeper understanding needed if despair would be avoided. As the underlying and unifying force of life, the human soul carries an inheritance of resiliency and a capacity for innovation in the face of disaster. When life becomes severely polarized, when people become alienated and isolated from each other, it is soul that has gone missing.

The modern world suffers a profound loss of soul not only at the individual level, but also at the level of community and culture. Because humans are secretly tied to the Soul of the World, the loss of soul not only diminishes the sense and meaning in human life, it diminishes and wounds the world. We are most lost and feel most abandoned when we have lost touch with soul, for it is the connecting force in life. Since soul serves as the underlying connection of all things, it has the power to move all things. Thus, soul is the primordial and primary source of meaningful change and true transformation. This time of collective upheaval and cultural loss is also the time of a struggle for the presence of the human soul and a battle for the Soul of the World.

RECOLLECTING SOUL

Though our suffering friend from thousands of years ago had to deal with personal issues and face a host of social ills, even in his desperation he knew he had a soul. Because of this awareness, he may have felt a greater freedom to approach the edge of life and death and question the meaning of existence; he knew his soul would take the side of life. At the time of his greatest personal doubt, the weary man could turn to a lifelong witness and answering voice that had a meaningful say in whether he lived or died. He instinctively felt and correctly imagined that his soul might know more than him about the core value and true aim of his life. In the fragments of papyrus that somehow survived the ravages of time, there is an answering voice that speaks for the necessity of living life fully and finding hidden potentials waiting to be revealed. The anguished questioning of life did not go unanswered; both the personal and collective troubles found a compassionate response from within.

The Ba-soul was held to be the hidden dweller and resident guide within each person. It was the spirit of individual consciousness in a person and also the deep-rooted source of one's unique way of being. As both a pre-conscious and subconscious pattern of potential wholeness, the Ba was said to include everything that makes an individual unique and one of a kind. The Ba was imagined to dwell within a person's heart where it remained connected to the inner dream of each person's life. In his hour of need, the scribe turned to his Ba-soul and it turned him back to his origins and the original potentials of his life.

The idea and image of an inner guide and life companion has always been important, not necessarily as an aspect of a specific dogma or creed, but as a primordial understanding of the inner nature of human life. Throughout the ages, people all over the earth have been instinctively aware of the existence of an inner presence or cohering center. The ancient Greeks called it a person's inner *daimon*; in India, the *atman* was deemed to reside at the center of one's being. Polynesian culture deemed *mana* to be the unique force in each life, and the Romans held that each child was born with a resident *genius* that acted as guiding and protecting spirit throughout the course of life.

Whether it be called the Ba or termed a daimon or an inner genius, the enduring message and core concept is similar: Because of the presence of an inner soul, each person is, by nature, a unique being. Each is capable of awakening to a sense of meaning and purpose in life and therefore, each can in some way affect the condition of the world. The notion of a unique soul or inner genius places imagination and a potential for renewal at the very center of each life, making each person a potential contributor to the ongoing creation of the world. The idea of contributing to the healing and renewal of the world is essential to avoid feeling powerless and helpless in the face of radical changes and worldwide upheaval.

The intensifying anxiety and collective fears in the modern world can be considered a spiritual crisis in which we must find a greater sense of soul or else become more isolated and alienated from our lives and subject to increasing feelings of hopelessness and despair. The counterweight to the fears and anxieties we face at critical times in life is found in the depths of soul within us. The inner soul knows what we so easily lose sight of, what our life is worth living for, no matter what trouble the world around us may be in. Although most of modern life is arranged to take us away from ourselves, the soul is always on the verge of some great awareness and on the edge of awakening to a more genuine way of being.

FROM THE SCRAP HEAP OF HISTORY

Although the story of the World Weary Man may be incomplete and remains inconclusive, it continues to speak to us of the abiding presence and guiding nature of the human soul. The final response of the Ba-soul to the feelings of being hopeless and helpless is to urge the sufferer to return to the moment of birth and "day of his jubilee." The solution to the dilemma of feeling that life might be at an end can be found by turning back to the beginning. Birth is not just the genesis of each person's life, but also the onset of the soul's unique adventure on this earth. In turning back to his origins, the World Weary Man once again finds the union of self and soul that can initiate a process of regeneration and renewal.

While the moment of birth is commonly seen as a miracle of life, the greater miracle may be found in the soul's capacity to renew life—and to do so when all seems lost or at an end. For, the soul stays connected to the eternal pulse of existence; it sustains the sense of life's potential even in the midst of turmoil and overwhelming cultural change. The soul is the core part of each person and the root of both individuality and originality. When everything seems to fall apart, the soul instinctively seeks to awaken and grow the original design that it carried to life to begin with.

A concept like the Ba-soul is more than a footnote in the tattered scrolls of ancient history. The Ba was the hidden dweller and inner guide, birthed with the individual and sharing in one's life from within. The sense of an inner soul capable of awakening in each person represents a pervasive and long-surviving force in human imagination and understanding. As with the myths of creation, where life seems to arise from darkness and emptiness, the origin of each soul remains the place of potential and thus the source of the instinct, as well as the energy, for life renewal. In the inner realms of spirit and soul, the beginning keeps trying to begin again. This kind of renewal involves a greater sense of individual presence and being; a being that is both more conscious as well as more purposeful in life.

From the tatters of time and the ravages of history, the answering voice of the soul speaks for the necessity of living fully—both despite and because of the troubles and injustices that plague the world. Written with a reed brush, weathered by time, and tattered by unseen hands, the scroll and its story have somehow survived for over forty centuries. Its existence seems to prove a point about the enduring nature of the human soul as well as its ongoing struggle to find meaning and purpose amidst all the disappointments, injustices, and tragedies that can be experienced in the course of life.

In dark times such as these, it is easy to become world weary and disenchanted with life. Yet, we are born to a particular time and must experience the awakening of our souls through the teeth of the time in which we find ourselves. Against the background of collective history, each person carries an inner plotline waiting to unfold. The soul must be lived to become known, both to ourselves as well as to others. As the lived "eachness" and vital uniqueness at the center of our lives, it contributes presence to the world and meaning to life. Like the old torn parchment that was long neglected and tossed on the scrap heap of history, the soul lingers nearby, waiting for the moment when the dust of life can be shaken off and the light of the soul can return to our awareness.

CHAPTER 2

INDELIBLE MARKS OF THE SOUL

Life must be lived forward, but can only be understood backward.

I found a translation of the tale of the World Weary Man at a point when I was trying to understand critical events that had happened in my life. The image of the soul keeping the weary man in touch with a sense of inner meaning and purpose helped me look more deeply into a dark and painful period of my own. Throughout my life, I have heard people say that we have to leave our troubles behind us and just move on. Over time, most experiences do fade from thought; however certain events stand out like signposts no matter how much time has passed.

I have found that the most important and often troubling events in life not only touch us deeply, but leave an indelible imprint on our souls. What marks us deeply also tends to indicate where the depths of our souls can be found. When seen as markers of the soul, the key experiences in life—whether deemed positive or negative, challenging or traumatic—can indicate where the core patterns as well as the latent potentials of our lives reside. Just as the old document of the World Weary Man has survived the ages and found its way into modern times, significant events from our past travel with us as well.

When viewed from the sense that each person is unique, each life can be seen as a distinct story trying to unfold from within, a living mystery trying to be revealed. Like any mystery, the trail of significant clues must be discovered and be thoroughly examined. Seen in this way, what marks us deeply can become a key for unlocking the secret of who we are at our core and what we are intended to be in this world. In the end, we can become more present in life, not less so, by facing our souls and examining the indelible imprints we carry from our past.

Looking back far enough, I come upon my younger self, alone and exiled. Not just far from home, but imprisoned in both inner and outer ways. In the outer world, I was in fact locked in a cell, confined night and day in a remote prison. Inside myself, I also felt confined and caught in a dilemma that seemed to offer no way out. Since the circumstances developed into a predicament I was not expected to survive, it became all the more an indelible, enduring chapter of my life.

I was not in prison for stealing or cheating or doing bodily harm to someone. I was in a military stockade, ostensibly for refusing to follow orders, but also because my soul seemed to require it. The trouble began when I was twenty-years-old and not sure what to do in life, not even sure that my life had really begun. It was a time of great social upheaval as all the fault lines throughout our culture were growing deeper and wider. The whole country was undergoing a period of radical change. Eventually, the collective soul searching was brought to a fever pitch because of the war in Vietnam.

At that time I had been working my way through college by loading freight on and off trucks on the docks in New York City. When it turned out that receiving an academic degree did not solve the question of what to do with my life, I simply returned to working as a teamster. To me, it was honest, physical work that also allowed me to reflect on "long thoughts" and continue to study on my own. Just as I felt I had time to figure out the next step in life, everything changed and life began to turn upside down.

The lottery system for being drafted into the armed forces had not yet started when I received a letter notifying me to report for induction. Although I knew the notice had to do primarily with the collective issues of the culture and the war, it was addressed to me, and so I felt the need to respond personally. I sent a letter back declining the offer to join the war effort. My objection rested on the basis that it was neither a declared war nor likely a just war. To me, there seemed to be no real sense to it and no good reason for it; so I wouldn't be attending.

Although I followed the news and read the arguments for and against the war, my initial reaction arose instinctually from somewhere inside myself. At that time, it was still early in the conflict; before the anti-war movement had become widespread, before college campuses erupted, before the tragic procession of caskets filled with young soldiers could be seen on television. Before the morass of the tragedy had become evident and the quagmire became undeniable.

Despite my instinctive reaction, I became deeply conflicted about refusing to serve. Being young, I was easily affected by social attitudes, as well as family and cultural expectations. I was subject to influence from friends, almost all of whom stood in favor of the war. My father made clear that I had to serve my country and all my uncles seemed to agree. Some of my aunts had served during the "great war" as well, and my mother simply stated that, "our sons have always gone to war."

I soon found myself in a painful crucible, caught between outer pressures and an inner voice that seemed to be trying to awaken me to a different life. While struggling with the dilemma of what to do, I began to feel increasingly isolated and alone. I did not want to be alienated from my family and did not wish to abandon friends, some of whom were volunteering to serve. I felt afraid to be deemed a coward by the standards of the world in which I had grown up. At the same time, I feared that I could lose my sense of self if I did not take a genuine stand on what was becoming the defining issue of the era.

At times, I knew clearly what I thought and how I felt; yet I did not fully feel the strength of my convictions. I had only glimmers of a genuine inner life and only hints of what it meant to be true to myself. I had no sense of what depths of anguish and despair would be required for me to follow the inner voice and sense of presence in my own soul.

As the time for submitting to the draft grew closer, I faced a choice of going to jail for resisting or entering the army and likely going to Vietnam. I did not know which fate I feared the most, as each seemed to signal the end of any life I had imagined. In the end, I gave in to the outer pressures; I succumbed to a fear of standing all alone in the world. With a heavy heart and doubting spirit, I agreed to appear for induction and soon found myself on a night train, in the middle of winter, bound for basic training at a fort in North Carolina.

Although I felt averse to uniforms and the constant regimentation, there were things I liked about boot camp and the subsequent jungle training in Panama. I valued meeting guys from all kinds of backgrounds and all parts of the country. The camaraderie that quickly formed amongst us—all of us facing danger—at times could be palpable and reassuring. The challenge to grow physically stronger and face up to demanding situations was compelling. However, I could not help but bristle at the repeated calls to serve what seemed to me a misguided sense of nationalism and exaggerated patriotism. I continued to feel that the war was not necessary and remained deeply conflicted inside my heart.

A DEFINING MOMENT

Old wisdom warns how inner conflicts that are not fully faced must be lived outside oneself as fate. The truth of this idea was about to become an explicit, indelible experience for me as I sat in an outdoor amphitheater during a company training session. The dilemma I carried inside myself came to a head as an army officer began trying to rally the troops with descriptions of the overwhelming power of the United States Armed Forces. At the same time, he railed against the Vietnamese soldiers, calling them "gooks" and nothing but Communist rats.

At one point, he began describing the kind of encounters we would experience once we were "in country." Working himself up, he tapped his pointer at a hilltop depicted on a large topographical map. The enemy was up there, dug in and firing down on us. We were the defenders of democracy and liberty who must take that hill at any cost. In a kind of fever, he declared that when the order was given to assault the hill, we would all go straight up into enemy fire, no matter what. If the man next to you falls, you "soldier on" until the enemy is destroyed and that hill has been taken.

Seeming a little breathless, he glared fiercely and commandingly at the audience of mostly draftees. I raised my hand and when he nodded towards me, stood and asked why wouldn't we call in air fire? If we were the most powerful, well-armed country in the world, why didn't we just flatten the hill with air strikes and avoid going straight up into the line of fire? It wasn't that I had some kind of bombing strategy; I just wanted to challenge what seemed to me like dangerous brainwashing.

The officer appeared shocked that anyone would question his order, even if it was given hypothetically. Pointing up to where I sat in the bleachers, he warned that if he ordered me to die for that hill, I would do it. That brought me to my feet again as I fired back that I would not accept an order to die, or to kill for that matter, unless I felt it to be just and appropriate. He fired back that I if I dared to refuse his order, he would shoot me himself. Before I could answer back to that, the sergeant of our platoon pulled me out of the crowd and along with others, roughly dragged me out of sight.

FEAR AGAINST FEAR

In that moment, the dilemma that had been boiling inside me became a heated conflict outside as an inner voice stated what had been trying to surface all along. The training officer had pointed directly, possibly intentionally, at the issue we were all facing. Up to that point, no one had fully expressed what in many ways was the underlying issue: the fact that we had given up the right to decide our own fate in life. As I was harshly and repeatedly told afterwards, I was no longer a civilian with the luxury of deciding things for myself. I had taken an oath at the moment of induction and was now a soldier and would have to follow orders. I would kill when ordered to do so and be willing to die under orders as well.

The confusion at the center of the dilemma had suddenly and, as it turned out, fatefully become very clear. Something that had been only vaguely present before had now made me stand up and would not let me back down. The source and the force of it did not simply come from rebelliousness or fearfulness. Rather, something inside me seemed to know me better than I knew myself. Although I would subsequently be called a coward and a traitor to the nation, I knew that if did not stand up at that moment, I would betray something deeper and more essential within myself.

At that time in my life, I did not fully understand and could only intuit what I now know to be an essential truth worth fighting for, no matter the odds or the circumstance. When it comes to the human soul, the real battle is the struggle to truly become oneself. Not the self that others might want us to be, not even the self that we might wish to be; but the deep self and inner soul trying to awaken at critical crossroads in each life. What matter if a person achieves the world if they fail to become themselves? What matter if we win the war, only to lose the battle to become who we are intended to be at the deeper levels of life?

Ever since I had received the draft notice, I had been afraid that I would do the wrong thing. I became conflicted about what was the right thing to do in the situation. It was not only that I was afraid of failing in the eyes of others. It was not simply that I was afraid of dying, although I certainly had that fear. What had now become clear was that I was also afraid of dying in the wrong way and of killing for the wrong reasons. I had begun to realize that going against my innate sense of self and soul was, in itself, deadly. I was afraid of dying and learning I had been not only in the wrong battle, but in the wrong story.

I had been deeply uncertain if the call to war should—or even could—be a genuine cause for me. That uncertainty was erased in a moment when the officer insisted that I would follow orders no matter what I thought or felt, no matter what I believed to be true or held to be meaningful. It was not just that I refused to blindly follow orders; I was touching on the difference between the soldier who obeys and follows orders and the warrior who serves not just a greater purpose, but something transcendent. But, I did not know that yet. I was also touching on something radical and ancient within myself. But, I did not understand that yet.

Deep within me, something had begun to awaken; something that had its own voice, its own sense of timing, and its own knowledge of where I stood on the issues of life, death, and what was worth fighting and even dying for. Whether I understood it or not, something in me knew definitively what I stood for.

Looking back over many decades that have passed since then, most things have faded or been forgotten. Yet that moment, and the punishing period that followed, stands out starkly and continues to live within me. It was not simply that taking a defiant stand had changed the course of my life. It was also that the sudden moment of standing up made me become, at least momentarily, who I already was at some core level. It would take me days to understand even part of what had happened; it would take months in prison to begin to realize the true nature of what was trying to become known inside myself.

THRESHOLDS OF DESCENT

The immediate result of announcing that I would not follow orders that went against my inner sense of justice produced two distinct responses from the chain of command. The first response was an onslaught of emphatic and at times hostile orders from practically every sergeant and officer in my company. If I hesitated even slightly about following an order, I would have to do multiple push-ups. If I outright refused an order, there would be a list of company punishments that usually involved cleaning kitchens and bathrooms, or digging trenches. From then on, when not performing some punishment or other, I was confined to barracks.

When it turned out that facing an endless series of menial tasks did not convert me to being an obedient soldier, a completely different approach developed. I was ordered to report to the office of the company commander. I was surprised to find him calm and almost sympathetic to my situation. He explained that he had met with his superior officers and they had come up with a plan that I should appreciate. If I would agree to follow orders, they would arrange to transfer me to an officers' training program. Once there, I could take advantage of my education and be trained for a role that did not directly involve combat.

Clearly, someone thought that a little reverse psychology would cause me to change my mind. If I was unwilling to follow orders, maybe I would like to be the person giving the orders. However, what was happening to me was more like turning inside out than simply having a contrary attitude. What had awakened deep inside me would not be easily pacified.

The captain seemed shocked and truly disappointed when I explained that a promotion would only compound the situation. There was no honest way that I would be able to give people orders that I would not want to follow myself. Inevitably, I would wind up back in the same dilemma. Rather than receiving a transfer, I suggested that it was time for me to leave the military altogether.

Not long after that, I received a series of court-martials and was informed that a time had been set for a military trial. A young lieutenant was assigned to aid in my defense, although he had little to offer and seemed afraid of getting involved. I also received access to a small library where I could prepare my own defense. For a brief period, I felt like I was back in college trying to write a paper or preparing for a test.

Unfortunately, the feeling of arguing for my release or even having some say in the matter was dispelled before the hearing began. My defense advisor told me that the outcome of the trial had been decided at the officer's club before the court even convened. I was to be given the harshest sentence they could impose and sent directly to a military stockade. The irony of being in an army, theoretically fighting for freedom and justice, while being denied a genuine hearing in court was not lost on me. A greater irony concerned the fact that when I initially appeared at the local draft board, I was given the choice of entering the military or going to prison. Reluctantly, I chose to enter the military only to wind up going to prison as well.

Although I knew the outcome of the trial beforehand, I did get to take the stand and laid out my arguments against the war and the draft to the military court. Preparing for the hearing helped me become clear about the issues of war and peace and how misguided I thought the collective culture had become. However, in no way did that work prepare me for the arc of descent into solitude and darkness that was about to begin.

An old idea declares that the soul requires an outer drama so it can reveal its inner pattern and full imagination for life. Clearly, I had found the outer drama and my soul had responded in its own way. The problem was that the drama was by no means over; in many ways, it had just begun. If I had known in advance all that would follow, I might not have taken such a radical stance. Only years later did I find the clarifying idea that what truly awakens our souls will take us much further down a path than we would choose to go on our own. In the meantime, I had been sentenced and transported under guard to a small prison in Panama.

SOLITARY TIME

When first entering the prison, I had to strip down completely and have all my bodily orifices inspected by guards. From then on, each passage out of the stockade and back into the cells involved the same demeaning procedure. While there were practical reasons for this routine, repeated exposure to it also served as a ritual of humiliation. On one level, being stripped down distinguished prisoners from guards and established who was in charge. On another level, it made clear that you had descended to a kind of underworld where you would not only lose the most fundamental freedoms, but also all rights to privacy and dignity. Behind the gates of a prison, you are stripped down to who and what you are inside.

Despite and because of all the restrictions, there was a lot of tension and drama inside the walls of the prison. And my arrival there only intensified the strain existing between the authorities and the prisoners. In prison, people give you orders all the time, and it wasn't long before my issues with following orders managed to become an issue for all involved. Eventually, I was further separated from everyone and sentenced to solitary confinement for an unspecified period of time.

There are ways in which solitude can be a liberating experience; yet enforced solitude tends to intensify both the feelings of being confined and of being abandoned. The limits of a solitary cell soon make clear that there is nowhere to go and no one to turn to. For a time, I felt vaguely anxious and afraid; although not sure if I feared being left alone or having to be alone with myself. On the other hand, once in solitary, I did have some sense of privacy and at times the guards would leave me alone. Except for obligatory showers after the other prisoners had gone on work details, I had long stretches of quiet time. Although not allowed to have books or other reading materials, I did have pens and a notebook. Eventually, I worked out a routine of writing and doing exercises while also imagining what I would do once I got out.

Alone in my cell one evening, I sensed that someone was watching me. I could not see anyone standing at the bars in front of the cell and could not tell where the attention was coming from. Finally, I looked up at the long bars that served as a ceiling for the row of solitary cells. To my shock, there was the captain of the prison, perched on the bars, staring down at me. It was a creepy feeling and I told him so. He told me that it was not the first time he had come there to observe me. He said he intended to figure me out before I caused him to lose his best opportunity to rise above the rank of captain.

As I looked up bewildered, he explained that Panama was not a big place and news could spread quickly. The story of a draftee in solitary confinement for refusing orders had circulated through the ranks of soldiers and officers alike. One result was a growing pressure on him to resolve the issue of having a war resister in the command. I told him there was nothing personal against him, but no matter how many orders I might receive, I was not about to change my mind.

To my surprise, he began to explain what he felt was his own dilemma. He said there were only two ways he could ascend through the ranks of the army. One way required that he volunteer to go over to the war in Vietnam, where people could rise quickly under battle conditions. The only other path he could see required that he run such an exemplary prison that he would be promoted for excellence of service.

Without seeming to realize any irony, he looked down at me and candidly stated that he had no intention of risking himself in the war. That left only the path of impressing the general who came to the prison for regular inspections. He felt he ran a clean and tight stockade. But the problem now was that everyone, including the general, was upset about the soldier in solitary confinement who refused to take orders. Thus, his greatest fear was that the general might blame him for not making me get in line and I would turn out to be the obstacle that blocked his career plans.

I could tell he was a calculating person, but I also became concerned that he might be somewhat paranoid. From his perch on the bars above, he asked all kinds of questions about my life. When he began questioning me about what I was writing, I simply said that the writing was personal and turned back to my notebook. When I looked up again, he was gone. He continued to appear up on the bars from time to time, sometimes in civilian clothes. He seemed to expect me to listen to and sympathize with his worries and career concerns. Despite his plan for getting promoted, he eventually admitted that he also felt imprisoned. He feared he would wind up in the little prison for his whole career. I could sympathize with that feeling as I had begun to have concerns about how long I would be locked up.

A DEEPER DESCENT

By then, everyone connected to the military knew the story of the strange kid who refused orders and was now in solitary confinement. Although officially I was not allowed visitors, a veritable parade of military officers began appearing at the door of my cell. At first, the issue seemed to be that my disobedience and refusal to follow orders threatened the very structure of their lives and everything they believed in. Each officer seemed to think that somehow he had the magic power to make me come to my senses.

Either he had the right reasoning or the ultimate way of giving orders, or else he could be threatening in a way that would change things with a single command.

At first, lieutenants and captains began appearing, eventually majors and colonels showed up as well. Each felt a need to come into the cell and give me an order, only to experience firsthand the process of having the order summarily dismissed. Initially, I was defiant and angry, matching their insistence with my own brazenness or contempt. Strangely, once they realized that I would not obey, most of them would sit down and talk. It seemed that once the exercise of giving orders proved futile, they experienced a need to converse with someone who was clearly outside the regular chain of command.

No one would state it outright, yet everyone somehow knew that I was in an unusual and unique position. Mostly they wanted to unburden themselves of something deeply personal, or even secret. One after another they would confess something that weighed heavily on their heart or their soul. Having been raised as a Catholic, I knew something about the ritual of confession. Somewhat reluctantly, I began to play the role of confessor and even spiritual adviser when the situation required it.

The truth was that although I could deny official orders with absolute confidence, I could not deny the unofficial requests for sympathy or even for forgiveness. What for me had started as a tough-minded stand, taken as a way of saving my own sense of self and soul, began to shift to a place of being more open-minded as well as open-hearted. On one hand, I could see the pain of those who otherwise were willing to punish and condemn me. On the other hand, I began to see the shape of my own life differently.

Somehow, I had gone from being called a coward and a traitor to being treated as a confessor and counselor. In a way, I had accomplished the goal of proving that I did not belong there as a military recruit. In the dark confines of solitary confinement I had unofficially and, as it turned out, temporarily been transformed from a soldier to a kind of priest or healer. It was as if at certain depths or at the extremes of human need, the ruling archetypes could simply shift or change places. From the deeper view of life, healers are just as archetypal, and likely more often needed, than warriors.

Had it been another era or in a traditional culture, the transformation might have been consciously acknowledged, might even have been confirmed and sanctified. Instead, I remained in a kind of limbo, a prisoner deserving punishment and rebuke on one hand, a private counselor or confidant and confessor on the other.

A MYTHIC INTERVENTION

As time went on, that was not the only paradox I experienced, nor were those the only visitors I received. At times I would sense a presence with me in the cell when no living person was there. Instead, I would see or hear characters from ancient myths. It seemed to happen especially in moments when I felt discouraged or overwhelmed with loneliness and sadness. Precisely when I began to feel that I had nowhere to turn, a character or a scene from a myth would appear before me. On one hand, I would be thankful for the strange sense of being accompanied by the "unseen." On the other hand, I was afraid that the isolation was getting to me and I might simply be seeing things.

Eventually, I recognized that the feelings of sadness and aloneness were similar to how I felt when I was thirteen and first realized how sad and disappointing the world could be. Growing up in my home, I could feel my father's depression as a both an absence and a kind of dark presence. I could see how my mother was overwhelmed by having five children and feeling trapped while also fearing that her life might be slipping away. Outside the home, things were tough and people could be rough. I sensed that most had lost their dream of life.

When, at the age of thirteen, I accidently received a book of ancient myths, another world opened up, as if I had found the real language of my life. The stories were full of challenges and adventures, but also depicted the harsh realities and penchant tragedies of life. There was an underworld into which people could fall by a sudden stroke of fate, by losing someone they loved or simply by virtue of feeling great sorrow. That mythic view of the world gave me more than a simple sense of hope; it gave me a deeper sense of imagination about the complexities and longings of the human soul.

Finding myself alone and trapped in another kind of underworld, it made sense that my psyche would turn to myth. What made less immediate sense was how the visions and visitations would completely alter my sense of awareness and challenge my sense of reality. In a strange way, I found myself facing another dilemma. On one hand, the visitations gave me a reassuring feeling that I was not completely abandoned despite being isolated. On the other hand, they could leave me unsettled and a little fearful of what might happen next. If the parade of officers looking for sympathy and understanding was odd and unusual, the appearance of mythic characters had me questioning whether I might be losing my grip on reality.

While I might serve as a confidant for others, under the circumstances, there was no one I could seriously talk with, much less confide in. I could not send or receive letters or research the subject of apparitions, hallucinations, or waking dreams. Except when I sensed the numinous presences nearby, I felt I was completely on my own. The question became whether I was losing my mind or actually finding it in some deeper way.

Like most modern people, I was educated to consider things in terms of logic and rationality. Yet, nothing I was experiencing during that time seemed rational or logical. The state of turmoil and war gripping the outer world seemed not only irrational, but pure chaos. And being imprisoned for following the convictions of my own conscience did not seem completely rational either. The rational world seemed far away and I felt I was falling further from it. At times, I felt like I was quietly falling out of life.

Like the World Weary Man, I had reached the end of what I knew and seemed to have hit the bottom of life. Yet, instead of finding a dead end or an endless void, I was actually on the verge of finding the ground of my own soul. Not having anywhere else to turn, I finally turned to the visions and promptings of my soul. I decided that my soul was sending me messages in the shape of figures, which I could recognize from stories that I had read repeatedly and found inspiring.

The truth is that the ordeal was not even close to being over. I would remain in confinement and come close to dying several times. Yet, something had broken loose with regard to the condition of being imprisoned inside myself. What had begun as an issue in the outer world had become a crisis within the far reaches of my soul. When all else was stripped away, what remained was a vital connection to imagination, a subtle bridge to something ancient and enduring that was an essential part of me. Take away everything and what remained was something indelible that could not be taken, even if I had barely recognized its presence before. Without fully realizing it, I had been in a struggle to find not just the voice, but also the true nature and aim of my own soul. Instead of falling endlessly into the void, I found myself landing on the ground of my being, near the roots of my soul. It seemed that because I had not given up on my soul, it would not give up on me.

CHAPTER 3

LIFE ON EDGE

The soul is the part of each person that
cannot simply be overwhelmed.

In the story of the World Weary Man, it is not an accident that the ancient scribe found himself caught between suicide and the soul. Soul is the connective tissue of life. If we lose enough connection to the cohering sense of soul, it can become hard to imagine that life has meaning or that we have a reason for being. When the World Weary Man says, "death is in my sights today," he names the third element in the ancient conversation with his soul. Thus, the scribe represents a person suffering life at the human level, the Ba-soul presents the possibility of reconnecting to his origins and birth potentials, and the presence of death invokes the power to either end or else radically change his life.

The Ba-soul responds to the feelings of helplessness and loss of self-worth by exhorting the man to embrace life anew. The Ba reminds him that only at the end of the journey does the real shape of one's life become fully revealed. There is an implication that if he dies in the wrong way, he will end his days separated from his own soul and there will be no place of rest or peace after death. Because ancient people imagined that the human soul existed before birth and continued on after death, such a tragic outcome used to be called a "fate worse than death."

The Ba-soul promises to stay with him even after his time of death has come. At the end of life they will travel together to the west. Since the human soul used to be viewed as an integral part of the cosmos, the natural course of human life was seen to follow the arc of the sun. After a time of ascension and visible brightness, the light of life enters a decline and descent into darkness. Since the west is where the sun sets and the light becomes swallowed by darkness, it was imagined to be the resting place of the ancestors, or the Land of the Dead.

Strangely enough, in ancient Egypt the deceased, who followed the path of the sun's descent, were called "Westerners." Some irony arises where an ancient term for the ancestors, those who represent the past, becomes a reference to "modern" people who tend to be obsessed with the future and are consumed with things that are bright and "new." Then again, the otherworld is nothing if not paradoxical. For, the west was also the place where life could renew itself, just as the light each day returns from the dark. In ancient Egypt, as in many traditional cultures, the realm of the ancestors was a place of necessary ambiguity that could be both the land of the dead and the place where life endlessly renews.

The Ba-soul represented the connection each person would naturally have to the otherworld. As the light hidden in the darkness, the Ba was often symbolized as a star that could guide a person through the troubles of life and the dark nights of the soul. *Destiny* means "of the stars" and the idea of each person being connected to the stars appears in cultures all over the earth. We may be small and insignificant, nothing but a speck of life in the great universe, but we each have a speck of star within us. The universal idea of an inner destiny depicts the hidden spark that connects us to the cosmos and makes us part of the swirling dance of stars and planets. The innate sense of a unique life aimed at something meaningful is the residue of stars and the inheritance of great imagination deposited within each of us.

In the deep interiority of the soul, the light of the stars fed the essence of each life. For something deep inside each soul is threaded to the stars and tied to the cosmos in ways that are both subtle and enduring. Everyone has an inner spark and speck of star, though it is more visible in some than in others. When it does shine forth, it reveals something different in each person; the spark of life is the uniqueness set within each soul.

Being born on earth means being "star-born;" it also means being star-crossed as we struggle to find the inner connections we each have to our mythical inheritance and genuine sense of purpose. The inner spark would light the way to a meaningful destiny in each life, yet it must find its fuel in the limits of the here and now and in the exact conflicts found in each psyche. It must shape the inner flame from the raw material of experience and from the burning questions that trouble our souls. Each person must learn the language through which the unseen world speaks to them or else miss their star and become lost in the storms of the world and the confusions of life.

By now, it may be more common for people to worry that a random asteroid might come crashing into the earth and destroy the whole planet. All the while, a great disaster is happening every day as people fail to connect to their own cosmic souls, the shooting star that entered the world when they were born. "Disaster," like "asteroid," is also a star word. A great disaster happens when we miss our star and follow the lights of others or simply become lost in the darkness.

This kind of cosmic confusion can happen more readily when the idea of a guiding inner soul has been displaced by the idea of an accidental universe. If we are born simply by accident, then our lives have no inherent significance or inborn purpose. Being the offspring of chance means our lives have little or no meaning. Not only that, but death also becomes meaningless, simply the dull conclusion to a random existence. In the modern world it is easy to feel both anxious and afraid. In addition, it has become easier to feel isolated and alone in the midst of all the unrest. It has also become increasingly common to question whether life is worth living at all.

SUICIDE AND SOUL

The gift of life comes to us with hints of emptiness and abandonment trailing along nearby. At times, the presence of the void can seem greater than the amount of presence in oneself. In such times a person needs an intuitive sense that the underlying soul is also nearby and that it knows better how to navigate the gaps in life and the depths of fear and sorrow. Lacking a sense of an inner guide or life companion, people more easily lose the sense of innate resiliency and an instinctive capacity to transform life. The loss of soul characteristic of modern life leads to a greater disorientation throughout the course of life.

Without a felt sense of connection to the otherworld of imagination and the inner world of soul, people can find themselves not only disoriented and unsettled, but also disconnected from the source of life. At the same time, we suffer a lack of holding images and loss of cohering stories that might offset the growing sense of worldwide uncertainty and existential doubt. There is a "collective trauma" as the hollowing of institutions and flood of rapid changes cause everyone to become more disoriented by the disruptive conditions of daily life.

As with the World Weary Man, feelings of despair and thoughts of suicide and death can arise because the time has come when we must change our life. Yet, lacking a sense that there is a greater self or soul within, the sense of a radical change in life can easily become confused with the idea of dying altogether; as if the longing for a connection to the otherworld becomes fixated on the land of the dead with no corresponding sense that the ground of renewal is also nearby. The idea behind many suicidal thoughts is not the need to leave this world behind as much as the need to leave behind certain ways we have been living in it.

"Suicidal ideation" is a modern term for the presence of suicidal thoughts and the condition of developing a preoccupation with death. The term itself indicates that when it comes to suicide, ideas matter. Whenever we feel we are in a "life and death" situation, our ideas about both life and death matter. The ideas that permeate the atmosphere in the communities and culture that surround us matter. And, because we are mythological and cosmological beings, the dominant ideas about the nature of the universe also affect how we think and feel about living and about dying.

When combined with notions of an accidental universe, the devaluation of the individual soul in modern life can lead to a sense of each life meaning less and less. It is one thing to suffer anxiety and feel the pull of despair; it is quite another thing to do so without the felt sense that there is also a knowing and sustaining presence inside oneself and that meaning and purpose are woven into the cells of our bodies as well as the depths of our souls.

Suicidal thoughts and feelings can often be an indication that a part of one's life has become inert or dead weight and needs to be shed in order for another life phase to begin. Sometimes seemingly self-destructive moods or behaviors intend not simply to destroy us but to clear the ground so that the unlived self can blossom from within. Sometimes, we must fall apart in order to re-collect essential parts of ourselves that we could not hold onto amidst early traumas in life. Yet, a modern person can more easily fail to understand that a part of them needs to die in order that they might find a greater sense of life. In confusing the part with the whole, people can take their lives by mistake.

A modern person, especially a young person, may have no idea of a genuine inner value or meaning when they encounter the kinds of isolation and pain that have become common in mass societies. Having worked with young people from all levels of society, I have learned how common it has become for them to feel that there is no inner soul or natural centering presence in them. Part of what they have absorbed from the cultural milieu is the idea of an accidental universe in which they are nothing but an accident themselves. The sense of human life being a random occurrence or a cosmic accident has filtered all the way down the social ladders and lodged in the minds of many young people.

Young people have always felt misunderstood; but increasingly they say that no one listens to them and that they do not feel seen. The connectivity of modern technology seems to offer a substitute for the process of being connected to and recognized by other people. However, people confuse simple connection with the crucial need to be truly seen and genuinely heard. What the soul longs for — and rightfully expects — is not simply to be recognized, but to receive confirmation of one's genuine self; not an automatic response from a device, but acceptance as a unique and valuable person. Despite and because of the omnipresence and speed of mass communication, young people can feel increasingly isolated.

Like the lamenting scribe, they can have no one to really talk to at critical moments in life.

There can be as many reasons for thinking of suicide as there are people who feel alienated or depressed, rejected, or simply uninvited into full participation in life. There can also be the kind of world weariness exhibited by the ancient Egyptian scribe who, though he lived during a simpler time, felt overwhelmed by collective levels of angst and despair. Young people can more readily become "world weary" because of a radical exposure to a world beset by enormous problems and seemingly endless conflicts, the news of which is delivered to them instantly through high-speed connections wired directly to their "personal devices."

Always connected but increasingly dissociated, people struggle to develop genuine presence and soulful connections in the midst of what can become a substitute reality. We are led to think that constant connection at a digital level will make us feel less lonely. Yet, the root of loneliness is the inability to be in deep connection with oneself. In an ironic twist, relentless connection can lead to a new kind of loneliness. We can be connected to anyone, anywhere, and at any time, yet also be more alone than ever before.

It can also seem as if all the underlying problems of the world have risen to the surface at the same time. Faced with massive climate changes and natural disasters driven by pollution and overpopulation, the proliferation of weapons of mass destruction, and religious battles and "culture wars" fueled by fundamentalist beliefs and a growing cloud of nihilism, we find ourselves questioning the meaning and purpose of life in a darkened way.

Without some sense of being "ensouled," people can feel empty inside and more prone to unconscious behaviors that can be self-destructive as well as socially disruptive. High-speed personal devices tend to feed into ego fantasies of being always connected and in control of one's personal world. Then, a sudden disconnect can feel like overwhelming rejection, a hard reality check can have dire consequences as the entire world seems to fall apart. Such a sudden disconnect can lead to a fascination with suicide or even homicide and mass shootings.

The tragic sense of personal annihilation can easily morph to a more global level and the conclusion that the world and the people in it must also come to an end. Loss of the sense of an inner soul that carries meaning and purpose can lead to a loss of life, even to the loss of many lives. Amidst all the worldwide high-speed connections, what most often can go missing are the soul-to-soul connections and the subtle sense that each living soul has inherent meaning and is secretly connected to the Soul of the World.

There is a point in the old papyrus scroll when the World Weary Man repeats several times that he feels "his very being is loathsome." Everyone has some experience of self-loathing, which can manifest as disgust with oneself and as hostility at oneself. Before reaching the deep places of self and soul, people can find themselves in an emotional territory that includes this sense of self-loathing, as if being near the center of the cohering soul requires encountering its opposite. The problem then becomes that if there is no confidence that the cohering center exists within us, the sense of self-rejection can dominate. When the distance between the ego-self or little-self within us and the deeper sense of soul has become too great, a sense of deep enmity begins to grow within us.

No one is intended to have a small or meaningless life; but everyone has the problem of the ego or little-self. The little-self represents more of an adaptation to early life conditions than a genuine orientation to the true purpose and meaning of our life.

This adopted and adapted self is "little" in the sense that it remains so much smaller and more limited than our natural spirit for life. Thus, the little-self can also be seen as a "false self" in the sense that it lacks the inner security and natural nobility of our underlying soul. Inevitably and repeatedly, the little-self proves unequal to the challenges and pressures we face in life. Yet, in believing itself to be the only self, it fears that letting go will lead to a great emptiness, a complete loss of self or even annihilation.

Despite major insecurities and sizable blind spots, the little-self insists on seeing itself as the ruling power of our inner life. Since the little-self began to form when we were but infants, it tends carry and maintain infantile attitudes. In order to maintain its rule, the little-self develops strong defenses and firmly fixed attitudes that limit our understanding of who and what we are intended to be in this world. The strongest defenses form in order to avoid our deepest fears and one of the deepest fears of the little-self is that underneath it all we may be empty or hollow. Thus, the problem with the adaptive solution to early life issues is that what first serves to protect us later block us from access to the underlying resources of our deeper self and soul. We must find a greater sense of self or become more isolated, divided and subject to increasing anxieties and feelings of helplessness and despair. The most common reason for despair and alienation comes from not being who we are at the core of the soul.

The human soul is ancient and resilient. At some ancestral level, it remains connected to the ground of being and the roots of renewal. By its nature, it encompasses much more than the ego or little-self can ever grasp. Unfortunately, it usually takes some challenging and fateful events for the little-self to let go and wake up to the true situation. Often we have to feel we are at the end of our rope or barely hanging by a thread before the shaky inner ruler will accept that someone or something else better knows what is needed. The little-self must admit to feeling overwhelmed by events and surrender its false notion of being in charge. Only then can we find the saving grace that is always nearby in the form of the innate wisdom of our own soul.

TO BE ONESELF

When the world becomes flooded with anxiety and uncertainty, everyone can have existential moments of severe doubt and despair. Everyone becomes world weary at times and each of us has an inner Hamlet who must repeatedly question the meaning and purpose of life. Yet, as the ancient scribe took pains to inform us, the question of "to be or not to be" is not as straight forward as it might seem. "To be" does not simply mean to act or just "do something." Nor does it mean, "I think, therefore I am." To truly be turns out to mean more than simply acting or just thinking. Each time the question becomes "to be or not to be," something essential and authentic is trying to awaken within us.

As fingerprints as well as footprints have always implied, human life exists in the particular, in the distinctive shape of the unique individual who bears an original soul within. Because each soul is by nature distinct from all others, it is each person's singular way of seeing and being that is ultimately at issue. Because each person born is a unique being, to truly "be" means to be as oneself, to act in authentic ways. The issue is not simply the question of life or death; the real issue is not being fully alive, for that is also a kind of death. Thus, the real question is to be or not to be oneself. As Emerson put it, "To be yourself in a world that is constantly trying to make you something else is the greatest accomplishment."

Typically, the dilemma of who we are is solved in too narrow a way. We limit ourselves to prescriptions of what others consider attainable and renounce the hidden potentials that our souls hint at all along. The problem is that we are each involved in a unique experiment and there is no formula or series of prescribed steps that can save us from the struggle to awaken more fully. The answer to the existential dilemma of being or not being cannot be found outside oneself. It is the unique inner life of the soul that needs to be found and become awakened within us.

Like the World Weary Man, we must be reminded of our true origins and learn to trust the deeper knowledge that we are not empty inside. Genuine empowerment involves a revelation of potencies and potentials set within us from the beginning. The deep self and great soul within each of us has innate nobility and spiritual fullness from the time of birth. If there is something genuine and irreplaceable hidden inside one's life, then each life can have its inherent inner worth, regardless of the circumstances of birth or the conditions of the world at a given time. Each person, regardless of birth status or orientation, can be seen to have essential nobility and meaningful life purpose based upon inherent inner qualities and deep resources of their soul.

The story written within the soul requires a drama of self-realization and self-revelation. On such occasions, the veil between the little-self and the deep self becomes thin and a self-adjustment becomes possible. If a person doesn't become paralyzed with fear or fragment into pieces, the deep self will rise to the occasion. Usually, it takes the right kind of trouble to move the little-self out of the way so that the deeper self can bring its resources forward. Something inside the soul knows the true aim and purpose of our lives; yet we must become lost in order to find it.

The deeper self is a living library with access to all the knowledge needed for living fully and growing wise. The ego visits the deep library of self at least occasionally or we lose all true sense of ourselves. The little-self is a creation of the deeper self even though it keeps forgetting that fact. When a life situation will abide no compromise, the little-self is intended to bow to the greater presence and innate knowledge of the deeper self.

When the knowing self takes charge a surprising sense of peace can occur, even amidst chaotic circumstances. At the same time, inner resources previously unknown become available to us. When the deeper self and soul manifests, we feel truly empowered, especially empowered to be our true selves. "To be" is to awaken to the thought held deep in one's heart and the imagination set in one's soul and, in that way, be as one was intended to be all along. In awakening to the inside story of the soul, we become the thought that intends to be brought to life through us, the living word that exists within and would be spoken into the world by virtue of our being fully present in it. The answer to the burning questions about the meaning and purpose of one's life turns out to be hidden where the origins of one's spirit for life and capacity for growth at any age can be found: in the ground of one's being.

CHAPTER 4

INNER EYES OF SOUL

Transformation is a fundamental law of the soul.

The time-honored saying that "the eyes are the window to the soul" is widely known. It has been attributed to the Bible, ascribed to Cicero and Shakespeare, and can be found in proverbs from around the world. As a key aspect of our body language, our eyes give us away and can reveal more about us than our words. At times people avoid "eye contact" because no matter what face we might put on, our eyes cannot lie. The sense that we can know a person simply by looking them in the eyes turns eyesight into insight. It also reinforces the idea that there is a specific soul, hidden within each person, which looks out at the world.

The lesser-known view about vision and soul involves the idea that a second pair of eyes exists in the depths of the human soul. Whereas the first pair of eyes opens shortly after birth, the inner eyes of the soul can remain mostly closed and concealed within us. The second set of eyes involves both psychological and spiritual capacities that can remain untapped until something awakens us more fully and truly opens our eyes. The opening of the inner eyes begins to reveal the true aim and natural path envisioned by the soul before we were even born.

Seen this way, the gift of eyesight can include a kind of "second sight" as well as the kind of visionary capacities once attributed to "seers." In many old tales, those who act as visionaries are shown to be blind or lacking sight when it comes to the visible world. Although they can see what others cannot envision, a kind of compensatory factor leaves them blind in other ways. Yet, there are also traditions in which the inner eyes open and allow a person to see more clearly in both the outer world and the realms of the soul. In this view of the human condition, we belong to two worlds and thus require two sets of eyes in order to view the entire spectrum of existence and perceive the intricate levels of life.

The inner eyes of soul can be mostly closed until something causes us to awaken more fully and begin to discover our own unique way of seeing and being a seeker in both worlds. At critical times, in both individual and collective life, it becomes important to see everything differently; not to simply adjust our view of things, but to genuinely see the world anew. The inner eyes of soul are connected to the uniqueness of each person; once opened, they give us not only our own viewpoint on life, but also our own worldview. Ancient traditions referred to this kind of awakening of the underlying soul as opening the eyes of initiation. A person who has found their own worldview could be considered to have become truly initiated into life.

Despite the loss of traditional initiatory ways and the modern tendency to deny the importance of an inner life, the human psyche reacts to radical alterations in life as if a life-changing initiation were underway. Initiation happens or tries to happen whenever the course, direction, or meaning of our lives changes dramatically. In that sense, initiatory experiences happen to us throughout our lives, yet are rarely recognized; leaving most of us with incomplete stories and unfinished rites of passage.

After the ordeals of being in solitary confinement and having visions that included scenes from ancient myths, I became deeply interested in stories that involved sudden awakenings and other initiatory elements. Over time, I collected many tales and began to realize that I was essentially guided by stories. It was not that I would choose a certain story and try to follow its shape or meaning; rather, I would carry stories with me, in the way ancient storytellers once did, and suddenly, one would come into my mind. Then, I would know that it wanted to show me something that I needed to see at that time and needed to learn about life.

Eventually, I became so full of stories that I had to begin telling them or else I would drown in them. It was in telling stories that I began to see as if with another set of eyes. It was and remains a wonder to me how a genuine story can reveal so much of the unseen world and at the same time, help clarify things in the common world and make life itself more meaningful. Stories are a way of seeing that can be revelatory, both for the teller and anyone who listens hard enough. Yet, unlike science or philosophy, stories don't try to simply make a point; rather, they tend to follow the paths of the soul, wandering and circling around what wants to be revealed.

One of the stories I carried around for a long time involved an orphan boy who was abandoned by his own tribe. The tale came from the Blackfoot tribe of the plains of North America. It begins by describing how over time the people had become very prosperous and lived with an abundance of food. Then, everything changed and it seemed as if Nature was taking away all their abundance and leaving them in hard times and in a poor state.

It was as true back then as it is now that the hard times press the hardest upon those who are already poor or have a low status in life. That was the situation for a young brother and sister in the tribe who happened to be orphans. Having no one to care for them, they suffered greatly when the hard times came. The brother suffered in a particular way because he was deaf. He could not hear what people were saying to him or around him or about him. As a result, people thought he was foolish, dim-witted, and somewhat worthless. The sister was treated more kindly, for she was bright and cheerful.

When one day the sister was adopted by a family from another camp, the brother had to live completely on his own. Left to fend for himself, the boy lived like one of the mangy dogs who roamed just outside the camp, watching everything, sniffing the air in hopes of food, but not coming too close for fear of being kicked. He kept his head down, lived on scraps thrown to the dogs, and dressed in frayed robes discarded by the poorest people of the tribe. At night, he slept alone in a small cave like an animal in a den.

One day, the people decided to move the whole village to another place that they hoped would be more prosperous for them. Soon, all the lodges were taken down, everything of value was packed up, and the whole village began to move down the road. The orphan boy was told to stay behind because they were seeking a new life and had no need for someone who was deficient and could damage their opportunities.

The boy could not hear what was being said, but he understood the message well enough. He watched as everyone left to find greener grass and a better life. He hung his head, barely looking up while living in the emptiness of the vacated village. One day, it dawned on him that if he remained in that hollow place, he would always be alone and an outcast. In that moment, his eyes opened and he could see his predicament clearly for the first time. He could see the cause of his isolation, but also could envision a tragic outcome if he remained a solitary outcast. Since he knew no other people, he felt that he had to try to join the tribe, whether they wanted him or not. So, he set off following their tracks.

Soon, he became frantic that he would never catch up and would lose them forever. The tracks were wide and clear and he began to run between them. At the same time, he began crying with the full realization of his state of rejection and forced isolation. With tears running down his face and sweat running down his body, he ran with all his might. At times, he stumbled and lost his breath, but he would not stop. As he pushed himself on, something suddenly snapped in his left ear. There was a sound like a crack as if something had fallen out. He continued running, but now he could hear things all along the left side of the path. He heard the wonder of birds singing as he ran along. Then, there was a snap in his right ear and something seemed to come out as well. From the right side he could hear the rushing waters of a stream. It was as if the musical sound of water rushed all the way inside him.

Soon, the orphan boy could hear all kinds of sounds. It was as if another world had opened up all around him. For the first time in his life, the boy laughed out loud. For the first time, he felt a part of things. He felt something like courage growing in his heart. He stopped panicking and began to run at a consistent pace. He felt he had a right to follow the trail which the people had taken. He felt like he belonged in this world.

As the orphan boy came near the new camp, an old chief saw him running steadily along and felt that it had been wrong for the tribe to abandon him. The chief called out to him and waved him over. To his great surprise, the boy could hear the old chief calling to him. He seemed to be inviting him to rest and eat something. Of course, the boy ate as quickly as he could, as he was not used to being offered food. He was not used to hearing words either, but now he tried to take in each word and understand each sound.

The old chief noticed the intelligence in his eyes and a new alertness in his manner and realized that he was neither stupid nor crazy. The more the chief looked at the boy, the more he liked something about him. He gave him more food and decided he would adopt the boy. He would teach him to be a good hunter and become someone who would truly serve the people. The boy had to struggle to grasp the meaning of the words of the chief and how they applied to him. Once he understood, the orphan boy began to weep again. This time his tears were a mixture of sorrow and joy.

The old chief could see that the boy was able to understand his words and that he had a depth of feeling and awareness. He thought how everyone, including himself, had been wrong about the orphan boy. As he observed the blossoming of the character of the boy, the chief realized that no one had ever given the orphan a proper name. The chief decided to name him Long Arrow because he could see a long arc of possibilities in his inner nature.

Once given a chance, Long Arrow proved to be a fast learner. Soon, he surpassed those of his own age in knowledge and in certain skills. Eventually, the boy who had been an orphan had a big vision that became important for all of the people of the tribe. After that he became a trusted leader and people would seek his view of things when the trail of the future became unclear. However, he never forgot how people can turn their backs on others and abandon them, either because times become hard or simply because they fail to understand someone else's nature. He never forgot the generosity of the old chief either, and Long Arrow promised himself that he would never turn his back on others.

AWAKENING THE INNER INITIATE

I carried the story of the orphan boy for years before ever telling it. It was only when I tried telling it that tears came to my eyes. I cried as I described how he was abandoned by everyone and left behind. I cried again as he began running after the people who had rejected him and made him an outcast. Of course, I cried when he finally found some recognition and was seen and valued for qualities that were in him all along.

It was clear to me and to most who heard the tale that we all have orphaned parts of ourselves; parts that feel rejected and left behind. In some ways, we are always trying to find that village where we can be accepted for who we truly are inside. That is the old story, how each individual desperately needs to be found valuable in ways that might easily be overlooked, even by family. Meanwhile, the collective needs exactly the inner gifts of all of its members in order for society as a whole to awaken to that which makes life meaningful, wondrous, and truly bountiful.

For me, the story was initiatory in that it came at a time when I needed to heal some of the outcast parts of myself. Simply telling the story could make me feel at least momentarily whole. I was especially taken by the moment in which the orphan came to realize that he needed the people of the village, even if they felt no need to recognize or value him. Even if he was able to accept being an outcast, he still needed to be seen and have his precise humanity confirmed by others.

A story is more like a territory than a document, more like a place we can visit and learn from. Once I had told the story, I found that I could sit inside it and be with the orphan at each critical point on his path. Of course, we can only meet a story with our own lives, and feeling his abandonment and pain meant actually feeling my own. The same was true when it came to feeling the intense longing that made him exert such a wholehearted effort to be fully present in the world. Despite all the neglect and rejection, he found something in the depth of his soul that wanted to live and become seen and known.

The longing the orphan felt not only pushed him out of his isolation, it also cracked him open so that he could hear and see the wonder of life for the first time. In that moment, he crossed a threshold and transcended all the feelings of inadequacy and fears of rejection he had carried for so long. As he let go of his fears, the world around him became a place of wonder. It had been that way all along, but he could not hear it, see it, or fully feel a part of it.

The story of the orphan's radical awakening to the wonder of the world and the surprise of his own place in it was, to me, a depiction of how one becomes initiated into their own life. Initiatory experiences inhabit the same deep psychic ground as birth and death. Instead of normal circumstances, we enter radical conditions that can precipitate a complete change of life while also revealing the originally intended character of a person. The person in such an awakened state used to be referred to as an initiate, someone experiencing a radical opening of the heart and the soul.

Due to the process of awakening and opening up, the initiate could be "in their middle" and thus become aligned with their true center and in touch with their natural nobility. The orphan boy, running between the tracks of those who abandoned him, begins to open up and find himself in the midst of creation. He is as if reborn — born again and born anew — having become able to hear with new ears and see the world and his place in it with new eyes. Then it can happen that those who have the eyes to see, such as the old chief, can perceive the true character and innate nobility of the soul trying to awaken. It is the moment of awakening that needs to be recognized and be blessed for us to be able to claim the true nature of our own souls.

The story of the orphan boy depicts a life-changing initiatory process that is not a formal rite of passage. The age of the orphan boy is not made clear and the radical changes begin in the absence of any sense of community. He is literally on his own when things begin to change and the changes begin deep inside his soul. Rather than the ceremonial forms that rites of passage might take, stories like this preserve and present the archetypal nature of initiatory change. Since most of the practices of initiation have disappeared from modern culture, it becomes important to understand the underlying energies and dynamics of this essential and enduring process of human transformation.

UNEXPECTED BLESSINGS

The human soul is timeless; it has no age and can manifest its nature at any time. Something in us wants to be fully present in life, even when the world around us prefers to deny or ignore the inner facts of our lives. In the same way, a timeless story can stir up key memories and old feelings. Like the orphan boy, core elements of our lives want desperately to become conscious to us and be recognized by those who can see and bless our inner way of being. Despite knowing that a mythic tale will stir pertinent aspects of our own stories, I did not see the connection to my own life at first. Yet, as I carried the story of the orphan with me, I found myself thinking about a particular time when I was a boy.

The memory that was stirred up had me back in a classroom at about eleven-years-old. My family had recently moved to the area and I was in a new school. Since no one knew me, there was a chance for different aspects of my personality to come out. At the same time, I found that old fears and concerns follow us quickly, no matter where we might move. One of my concerns involved not knowing where I fit in with my peers. I knew I did not fit with those who try to be perfect or follow all the rules. Yet, I didn't want to be someone who was cruel or did harm to others.

My new class was in a nearby Catholic school and our teacher was a young nun. She was also new to the school and may have been in her first year of teaching. She was round-faced and kind of portly, although the latter was more of a guess as the habit she wore was loose enough to obscure her actual body shape. We liked her more than the other nuns because she smiled openly and welcomed us to class each day. In a situation where there many rules and the teachers were strict, she seemed emotionally present and even sympathetic to our plight as students.

The classroom was divided in two with the girls sitting on one side of the center aisle and the boys on the other. Besides being separated by gender, the students on each side would be arranged according to the grades achieved on the most recent report card. Those who had the highest marks sat at the front of the class, closest to the teacher. Those with the lowest grades sat toward the back. Since grades were also given for behavior and cooperation, the seats at the very back of the room were reserved for those who misbehaved or disobeyed.

A problem developed shortly after we received our mid-term report cards. As it turned out, I had qualified to sit at the head of the class due to having the highest grades. At the same time however, I also merited the last seat as a result of bad behavior. Based upon the policies of the school, the bad behavior carried more weight than the good grades. So, I was placed in the backmost seat of the last row of boys. The next morning, right after prayers at the beginning of class, the sister announced that there was a problem that concerned everyone in the class. She was clearly emotional and seemed to search for the right way to describe the problem that affected us all.

"Our Michael," she said, nodding toward me at the back of the room, "has the highest grades and should be sitting in the first seat. But because of his acting up I am required to make him sit at the back of the class. When I brought the issue up to Mother Superior, I was told I also had to punish him so he would behave in the future." At this point, she struggled to hold back tears. "I have three brothers that I love dearly and miss sorely because we must live in solitude here as nuns. I would not want anyone to punish them or hurt them. And, I will not punish Michael as he could be any one of them."

By now she was crying openly, but also carrying on. "It is clear to me that Michael will either be a leader for the good or a leader for the bad. Because we want him to be a leader for the good, I will not treat him in a way that I would not treat my brothers. So, no matter what anyone says, I am moving him to the front of the class."

As I struggled to understand what she meant about leading and how I should feel about being singled out, something even more shocking occurred. The good sister suddenly pulled off her veil. We had never seen a nun without a head covering and were shocked to see that she had a very short haircut that made her look bald. She rubbed her head as if to clear her frustration over both the way her hair was cut and how it had to be covered up.

Still teary-eyed, she began to speak about how lonely she felt in the convent and how she had to be humble all the time; how she had to take orders from older nuns and priests and had no one to talk with. We were all shocked to see her partly defrocked and hear her lament in such an emotional, forthright way. The entire room was filled with emotion as she concluded by insisting again that no one could make her punish children in ways that were harsh and against her true feelings.

Although I was still unclear about what was happening, it was clear that I had to move to the front of the class where she stood in the midst of her courage and tears. As I walked past her, she kept nodding as if to encourage the part of me that might do some good. I felt very awkward and confused at the time, but looking back I can see that she was sincerely trying to bless my soul. She accurately intuited that I was the kind of kid that could turn out either way. More than being a nun in class, she was being a forgiving older sister. More than that, in taking off her habit and baring her own soul, she manifested an authentic presence and a kind of inner authority rather than a formal position. Her caring and courage affected all of us, even if we couldn't explain it at the time.

Her willingness to stand in the depths of her feeling and be honest with us transcended the fact that we were but children; it transcended the division that separated the girls and boys and erased the idea that we could be simply measured and ranked. She took a risk for the sake of all of us. In that sense, she was being like the old chief in the orphan story who did not want to allow a serious mistake to continue.

That lesson stands out more than having my wrists struck with rulers for writing with the wrong hand. It stands out more than having to bend over a desk after school to receive blows from a strap or being made to sit alone in silence for speaking during class. I can still see and feel the intensity of emotion that both overwhelmed and energized the young sister and the effort she made to be true to her own sense of self.

I did not know if what she was saying about me was true; but I wanted it to be. It touched something inside me that I did not yet understand. For me it was revelatory, as I felt complete empathy for her plight of not being seen or respected. Yet, at the same time, I felt truly seen; not just respected, but for a moment, possibly understood. Because she saw something in me, something of which I was barely conscious, I felt a greater sense that I had something to live up to in life.

THREADS OF INITIATION

Although some of the kids saw me differently after that, I can't say that the event changed my life on the outside, though it certainly marked me on the inside. Radical experiences in adolescence and early youth can prefigure elements of an inner plotline that only becomes clear in the passage of time. I can follow a thread from that day in class when the young nun took off her veil and wept and refused to punish me to the day I stood up and refused to take orders in the military. Knowingly or not, she was blessing something she could see in me that was also something that she was fighting for in herself. If I follow that thread farther, it leads to the day I decided to work with youth who were in serious trouble and in danger of losing their lives or at least their freedom.

When I started working with girls and boys who were severely at risk, both the courage to stand up for someone else and the idea of blessing younger people came back to me. In order to be helpful to youth who were in trouble, I had to empathize with them, no matter how they behaved. And, in order to be able to bless and encourage them, I had to have a place within myself where I, too, felt seen, blessed, and encouraged. In many ways, we can only mentor others to the degree that we have been mentored ourselves. We can only bless others if we have received some blessing and some healing in our own lives.

What initiates us marks us indelibly and what marks us can help initiate others. If we take off all the coverings we must wear to play our roles in daily life, what remains are those things that marked us and blessed us and continue to make us who we are inside. Certain events touch and confirm our "inner realities" as if there is an inner gradient or "through line" waiting to be found and followed. Besides the more predictable stage of life transitions, there are critical moments when we don't choose what happens, but we become the ones chosen. We are condemned to suffer in some way or receive unexpected rewards; we are elevated above our station or pulled into depths we would not willingly choose. Something unseen and unexpected touches our lives and we are changed in ways that can take time to unfold.

As the inner dynamic of transformation, initiation means the continuous breaking open of areas of the soul to reveal hidden capacities and inherent gifts. When life pulls at us from the outside and the soul pushes us from the inside, we reach the point where pain and longing requires that we change. A true turning point in life threatens one's habitual ways of being or acting on one level, but also opens the doors of perception at another level. We come to see the world as we are intended to see it and awaken to the true aim of our soul. As in the orphan's story, initiation involves healing old wounds as well as revealing the unique project of one's inner self and soul.

After being prefigured in adolescence, initiation is the psyche's instinctive response to both the severe struggles and the great opportunities found in the course of life. Success as well as failure can shift the psychic ground in a person and any break, loss, or severe separation can evoke the sense of initiation in a person's psyche. Whatever interrupts, breaks us open, or breaks us down— whether it is the trauma and shock of a loss in life or the drama and exhilaration of success—also initiates us into a greater knowledge of ourselves, particularly knowledge of the nature and style of our given soul.

Life is change and the life of the soul is transformation. An initiation involves entering a threshold where we can gather enough tension and momentum to push ourselves to the next stage of our life. In that sense, initiation not only means taking a new step on the road of life, but also undergoing a complete change of life. What initiates us also strips us down to the inner essentials and releases qualities and powers that were hidden within. Thus, stepping onto the path of initiation also means that there is no going back. On the path of transformation, there can be no way back to the self-identity or sense of life we had before.

Whatever alters the overt patterns of our lives also opens us up to psychological and mythical levels of unusual depth. Accident, divorce, abortion, the death of a loved one, the loss of a career, even eruptions of nature which destroy and reshape the landscape, all can precipitate the psyche's expectation of a thorough rite of passage. They are the detours from the mainstream that keep our hearts open to growing and our minds open to learning who we are and what we are meant to do in the world.

Using a "psychology of initiation," experiences that change our life and mark us as individuals can be opened up and re-examined to learn what tries to live into the world through them. Seen through the "eye of initiation," the exact wounds we carry turn out to be openings to a greater imagination and deeper understanding of the life-changing experiences that truly make us who we are in life. The real work of life involves meaningful attempts to rediscover the doorways that open the human heart and the territories of the soul. As a poet once said, I would give all the wealth of the world, and all the deeds of all the heroes, for one true vision.

An old idea suggests that each person comes to life at a time when they have something to give to the world. That sense of soulful giving may be more needed now than ever before, as the world needs genuine vision as well as great imagination to initiate meaningful changes in all areas of culture and nature. Strangely, it tends to be the orphaned and neglected parts of our souls that are the least known but can become most able to see what is needed on both the individual and collective levels of life. In order for our true callings and genuine visions to become known, we must become both open-minded and open-hearted. As an old proverb makes clear, "Whoever remains narrow of vision cannot be big of heart." We live in times of widespread trouble and sweeping change; if we can trust the nature of our own souls and throw ourselves wholeheartedly into those things that truly call to us, these could become initiatory times as well.

CHAPTER 5

THE PRISON WE ARE IN

A culture is a totality of imaginative power.
- William Blake

Shakespeare wrote: "There is nothing more confining than the prison we don't know we are in." In other words, whatever we are not conscious of can have a deep hold on us. In critical moments, we can wind up doing its bidding while believing we are making our own choices in life. We are in just such a prison of our own making when we act as if the common world of fact and figures is not only the "real world," but also the *only* world.

The prison of the modern mind is partly created by the common belief that "reality" can be limited to logic, statistics, and provable facts. Not that the literal world is "unreal," rather that it is the first level of reality and can never depict all that is truly Real. Restricting all modes of presence to a single plane of being leads to being trapped in a narrow view of life and imprisoned in the linear trap of time. Too much "hard reality" and the world becomes as if flat again; we lose touch with all that makes this earth a place of wonder and beauty and hidden possibilities.

Our world is a reflection of our own soul. Because we have learned to deny the world its soul and therefore its connection to the divine, it, too, can seem to be dying. Under the spell of literalism and the tyranny of facts and statistics, the modern legacy becomes an increasingly diminished world that has been overly quantified as well as thoroughly exploited. Materialism goes hand in hand with the sense of literalism, which reduces everything to the simplest matter, or the lowest common denominator. Instead of wonder and awe at the multiplicity of life and continuing surprise of existence, ideologies and fixed beliefs leave people enthralled with a single idea or a one-sided, single-minded way of viewing the world.

The rise of literalism signals the loss of imagination underlying both the fixation with measurable facts and the fundamentalism of fanatic beliefs. Literalism reduces the world to fixed ideas and rigid dogmas while isolating people at extremes of thought, feeling, and belief. Literalism takes the mystery and the natural sense of awe out of the world and eventually takes the meaning out of life. If there is no otherworld of spirit and imagination, there can be nowhere to turn when the real world becomes disorienting, when everything around us becomes both more irrational and increasingly chaotic. When life has lost its wonder and nature has lost its living halo, imagination is the missing ingredient and the necessary remedy for the disease of literalism.

NO OTHERWORLD, NOWHERE TO TURN

The way out of the mounting troubles that threaten and entrap contemporary cultures cannot be found solely by trying to understand history in order to not repeat it. For, it is not just that certain damaging things have been done in the course of time. The greater issue may concern the fact that so much has been lost and forgotten over time. The issue is not simply correcting the past, but learning to see the present world with different eyes in order to see it anew. Reality has always presented more than what simply meets the eye. The "known world" has always been the place of surprising visions and revelations, just as the great Unknown has always been the companion of the living. Where reason fails and logic stumbles, myth waits to open paths of imagination and understanding.

Before modern times, it was commonly considered that there was another world right next to the domain of facts and figures, and that this "otherworld" was also real. By insisting on one way of seeing or holding a single idea about "reality," we lose the subtle connections and miss the bridges that secretly hold the two worlds together. As an old saying would remind us, whoever can see no other world than the common one is truly blind. It is a terrible thing to see the world yet have no vision.

We live in a time between times, amidst a past fast disappearing and a future that often appears to be darker than anything we have known before. The betwixt and between quality of time has become more revealed as we find ourselves in a "liminal space," where endings and beginnings exchange rapidly and nothing seems clear and certain or fixed in stone. Call it apocalyptic time or initiatory time, for it is both. The times can be considered apocalyptic in the sense that everything seems on the verge of collapse and in need of renewal. At the same time, when in the throes of trouble, it is the nature of the human soul to awaken in ways that are initiatory as well as revelatory.

The heart of humanity has always dwelled betwixt and between, between the throes of hard reality and the wonders of great imagination. We are most human when in touch with the dream of life and the ongoing story of the world. The trouble is that genuine visions of healing and transformation tend to awaken only after more rational and familiar ways of seeing the world have failed.

Ultimately, the problems we face cannot be solved at the same level at which they were created. The current problems of the world are bigger and more complex than the institutions established to deal with them. Meaningful change requires a true transformation that shifts the levels of understanding and opens the realms of possibility. Yet, there is a poverty of imagination when it comes to facing the size and depth of the problems we all face. In mistaking appearances for the real thing, people wind up with the appearance of strength, the appearance of leadership and the appearance of meaning while suffering a loss of all that is truly meaningful in the end. Genuine change, whether it be in the hearts of people or in the culture at large, is more difficult than changing the appearance of things and therefore can be a more rare occurrence.

In hard times, inner changes must precede changes to outer circumstances. The "saving grace" for the modern prison of literalism and nihilism can best be found in a movement toward the visionary capacities of myth and imagination. The otherworld exists as the inner territories of heart and soul, as the realm of imagination and dreams that can renew us as well as help sustain life. The otherworld, which can also be experienced as the inner world, turns out to be the source of everything that people consider to be the real world. In the end, we either develop pathways to a true awakening of the soul or we add more bricks to a prison of our own making.

NEWTON'S SLEEP AND AWAKENING THE SOUL

During an earlier era of troubling change, the visionary artist and poet William Blake wrote, "Pray God us keep / From Single vision & Newton's sleep!" Blake instinctively opposed the view of the world being derived from Newtonian physics that leaves us in a mechanistic, unfeeling, and forsaken universe. Arising at the onset of industrialization, this narrow, literalized vision led, not just to a limited sense of human life, but also to a deadened sense of the world. Rampant materialism and "false objectivity" make the world impersonal, unimaginative, and empty of the mystery of presence.

In the face of mindless industrialization and dehumanizing objectification of earthly life, Blake argued that whatever exists must first be imagined. Drawing upon the age-old traditions of the seers and prophetic poets, Blake equated single vision with a poverty of spirit and a loss of imagination. He referred to those who live in the diminished realm of measurable reality as being trapped at the lowest level of consciousness. Having such limited views, they are inclined to become blind consumers on one level, but also be single-mindedly consumed with control and power over others as well as a desire to dominate nature.

Today, simply being alive means to become a witness, willing or unwilling, to the loosening of the web of nature as well as the unraveling of the fabric of culture. It means to be present as accepted patterns dissolve, institutions become hollow, and uncertainty comes to rule.

A new version of the sleep of single-vision, and a prison of our own making, appears where modern people, aided by mass media and technological devices, tend to retreat into their own world. Modern technologies allow a person to remain within an echo chamber, or feedback loop that reinforces whatever biases and fixed beliefs they might have. In the horizontal realm dominated by the internet and social networking, the world has become as if flat again. It has lost the vertical dimensions that were once inhabited by spirit and soul. In such a reduced world, anyone with genuine sensibilities and sympathies will naturally feel exiled and alienated.

Meanwhile, those who remain single-minded also become

simple-minded and increasingly subject to personal delusions as well as a flood of conspiracy theories. Assisted by technologies of isolation and encouraged by the politics of identity and division, people suffer increasing states of dissociation as well as extremes of emotion and fanaticism. In the midst of high-speed technological connections, we lose the vertical imagination that allows us to feel truly connected to our soul as well as to the Soul of the World.

Secretly, each soul is naturally gifted and aimed, but most aspects of modern culture serve to take us away from ourselves and help us avoid the very paths our soul would have us take. On one level, there is a body soul that has been invested with the breath of life; but there is also a greater soul within, one that has been invested with its own worldview and capacity for inspiration that can often remain asleep. Without inspired experiences that open the inner eyes and awaken the soul to such a double vision, a person remains one-sided and can become single-minded.

Having a one-sided view of life keeps a person in a kind of self-generated prison where they become both the inmate and the prison guard. Not only do they fail to find a way out, to a greater sense of life, but they also refuse to let anyone in. One of the greatest sorrows of life, that may be growing greater, involves how many people fail to live the life to which their soul aspires. All the while, the dream of our life keeps trying to awaken us from the sleep of the daily world.

Blake's plea is also a prayer asking for protection from the kinds of reductionism and literalism that leave us in a wasteland, cut off from nature and bereft of genuine insight, distant from the lights of both compassion and wisdom. For, a true vision must lead to an open heart as well as an open mind. Opening the eyes of the soul helps create a pathway between the mind and the heart, revealing the thought hidden within the heart.

The increasing pressures and threats found in the outer world create a tension that can only be relieved through a change of awareness from within. Amidst massive uncertainty one of the few ways to find sense and meaning is to awaken to the inner order, the shape and style of one's own being. The frequent statement that we need a "wake-up call" indicates that people know in some way that a greater state of awakening is not only possible, but is calling to us. We are intended to awaken to a call from a deeper ground of being as well as from a higher state of awareness.

Another way to describe the one-dimensional vision — the lowest state of consciousness — is the un-awakened soul. The first state of awareness, which many now call the "real world," appears as the common sphere of literal events, linear time, and measurable things. This state can also be referred to as the "waking world," especially when compared to being asleep and, in a sense, "dead to the world." Yet, to be only in the waking world is a kind of sleep as well, as many people can be seen to be sleepwalking their way through life.

It was also Blake who stated, "If the doors of perception were cleansed everything would appear to man as it is, infinite." He was drawing upon ancient ideas found in both Eastern and Western traditions that place humanity in a tension that stretches us between time and eternity, in a state that places us between the common ground of earth and the infinite reach of the heavens. Some see the place of awakening as a higher state of mind; others prefer a transcendent realm of spirit. Yet, several ancient traditions imagine the third state as an intermediate realm, a place betwixt and between the opposing spheres of time and eternity. This in-between state of existence involves neither being asleep nor simply being awake; rather, we enter a state of continuous awakening which combines and entwines the other two.

When in touch with the intermediate realm, we become able to see into both the evident world of time-bound things and the far reaches of the eternal. Each moment of true awakening is suffused with knowledge of this world and the wisdom of the otherworld, and such knowing holds the two worlds together, allowing imagination and inspiration to flow from the eternal into the time-bound world. Since the awakened soul turns out to be ancient and spontaneous at the same time, it allows us to escape the trap of history as well as the sleep of the unknowing.

In the dark times, the awakened soul can become the unifying agent for a collective renewal as entering the moment of crisis and living more fully parallels the spiritual passage from ignorance to illumination. Thus, the underlying soul has been called "the light hidden in darkness." It can also be termed the light of the deep self within, as it was in a passage from the Upanishads, one the oldest documents on the nature of humanity. In this ancient manuscript, a wise sage addresses the issues of what to do in the dark times. He is being questioned at the court of a powerful ruler who understands the material world but realizes that at times a deeper knowledge of existence is required.

Beginning with what he knows best, the king asks the sage, "By what light, do human beings go out, do their work and return?"

"By the light of the sun," answered the sage.

"But if the light of the sun is extinguished?"

"Then, by the light of the moon, they will go."

And so question and answer proceeded, each exchange leading to a darker place: If the moon is extinguished, then by the starlight; if even the stars are cancelled, then by the light of a fire. "But, what if the fire of life is in danger of being quenched? What then?" the king finally wants to know. "By the light of the self," is the conclusive reply of the sage.

Moments of true awakening are also times of greater enlightenment. The light that burns within us is also the light that dwells within everything; it is the hidden light at the center of all things. When the inner light of soul awakens us from within, something also comes alive in the world around us. That is how things change, from the inside out; from the soul to the world as the individual soul helps creation to continue. Our real gift to life involves an awakening of our inner purpose, for that is the star of our true destiny. When we are aware of life's purpose, the light of the soul shines into the world and the secret hidden within us becomes visible and encouraging to ourselves and to others.

Outside the process of awakening to who we are intended to be in the world, we easily fall into the common trap of seeing life from a material perspective. We become single-eyed and single-minded as what comes to matter most are simply material things and the predictable pattern of gathering more and more of what we do not really desire. Then, alienated from our own soul, we become increasingly alienated from creation and lose the deeper meanings of both individual and collective life.

WORLDWIDE WAKE-UP CALL

The fear of things going wrong blinds us to the fact that so many things have already gone wrong. We are already in the world that we feared might come. For many forms of life on earth, the worst catastrophes are already taking place. This is not the time to abandon the earth; rather it is the time to bring all kinds of inspired ideas and creative forms of imagination to aid both nature and human culture. At this point in the history of humanity, it is unlikely that there can be a single idea or sole system of belief that will save us from the accumulation of collective troubles and tragedies. The overwhelming problems and massive threats are global in scope, but they also function as a cosmic wake-up call, intended to awaken us from the sleep of so-called "reality."

Because all things turn out to be interconnected, the transformation we are going through is not a single change. Rather, it is a cascade of ceaseless change — a genuine transformation of the world. There is no way to simply think our way through our current predicaments. Although clarifying issues can help, there is no magic bullet, singular solution, or technological fix. There can be no "work-around" when the issues are too big and too complex to ignore or slip past. When the trouble becomes widespread in both realms of nature and culture, it is time to face up to what has been building up for a long time. When the world goes upside down, those things that are most important in life can slip from our grip and seemingly fall out of reach. When essential things become lost, we must look for them in the depths of the soul.

As an era comes to its end, the modern world finds itself at a crossroads that many cultures have entered before. At such times, the basic energies and underlying oppositions of life become more raw and exposed. The result is an existential crisis when it comes to understanding the role of humanity in the world, and an increasing loss of soul when it comes to caring for others and the earth. It is not just that we are mired in the kind of quicksand made from years of political expediency. It is not just that income disparity has become scandalous and dangerous to the welfare of entire societies. It is not just that the number of displaced people, refugees from war, and hordes of political immigrants have reached overwhelming proportions. It is also that we have lost something essential to understanding the meaning and purpose of human existence.

We are in such a radical churning of existence that life can turn upside down in a moment. We live within an ongoing tragedy, amidst the battle for truth and a search for meaning. In the maelstrom of such existential turnings and churnings, rationality tends to falter and faith can wither. At the same time, something meaningful and enduring about the world is trying to be remembered and be rediscovered, and it seems to take some big trouble to awaken to it. Eventually, the moment in time comes when it is necessary to make the unconscious conscious, at the collective as well as at the individual level. When it seems that everything is at risk it is the totality of the individual and of humanity as a whole that must awaken and respond to the call.

The transformation being sought must radically shift our collective awareness and our understanding of the role that humanity can play on this troubled earth. In that sense, the wake-up call is for everyone. Yet, what awakens and answers the call is the inner spirit and unique presence of the individual soul. The point cannot be that everyone learns to see in the same way; that would precipitate a new form of collective sleep. Therein lies the problem with all the "isms" that claim to solve all the problems, but which cannot affect a genuine awakening. It is the individual soul that bears the dream of life and must awaken to a greater sense of imagination and creativity. What changes the soul can change the world and do it without requiring that people simply agree or learn to see things the same way.

Certain rites of passage require that everything must first seem upside down, completely backwards or devoid of meaning before a step or a leap into the unknown can stir the soul and inspire the dream of life to awaken again. The status quo must seem about to collapse altogether in order that the esoteric or inner realm of soul might awaken again. Central to the sense of a collective initiation is the notion that imagination, not reason or will power, will once again be understood to be the primary faculty of the soul, its greatest power for making change. As the collective sense of unity collapses, the uniqueness within individuals becomes an essential source of unifying imagination. The inner myth becomes our individual connection to the world as well as our secret connection to the heart of Nature.

The world in which we live is not simply accidental, nor is it a neutral place; rather, it is a place of delicate symmetry. At this point in time, a coincidence of factors has made the balance of the world more precarious and brought us to a cosmic tipping point. The disruptive character of our era, which may not be of our conscious choosing, is nonetheless the context in which the individual soul tries to awaken more fully. Either we awaken to the wisdom and resources of the soul or we unwittingly contribute to the depreciation and further dissolution of the world. We are attempting to reconcile the age before it ends; we are seeking to "strike some balance," find some psychic poise, before the light closes on the era.

Despite what some might think, humans are not simply an accident of existence or an experiment that has run its course. Humans are a risk taken by the forces of creation in the interest of bringing conscious awareness and liberating insight into both the failures and triumphs of existence. The individual soul can be seen as a microcosm, a little world and realm unto itself. If penetrated deeply enough, it turns inside out and becomes a living thread to the Soul of the World. The Uniqueness woven into each soul acts as a mythic umbilical cord that remains connected to the otherworld and is the surest way of finding it, again and again.

Each person carries a hidden poetic unity that reflects the mysterious continuity of the Soul of the World. In the depths of the soul, we are each an old soul able to survive the troubles of the world and contribute to its healing and renewal. The key to what we miss and secretly long for is hidden within us. Medicine men and healers of all kinds from cultures around the world have used various techniques to not only "heal" the soul, but also to restore individuals to their proper place in the world and in their culture. To *heal* means to "make whole," and when we feel whole we are in touch with the whole world. When in touch with our underlying soul, we are naturally in touch with nature and the Soul of the World. We are the missing ingredient in the solutions needed for all that ails us, if we but awaken to the nature of our own souls.

When we awaken our souls, we liberate the divine spark that was there at the beginning of our lives, the true gift of life that is also light—the precise gift intended to be given back to the world. Awakening to one's life-story and finding initiatory paths comprises the "real work" and genuine opus of our lives. By the light of the soul and the inner eyes of initiation, we see life differently, see it all anew. Then, a sense of wonder and awe returns as the veils lift and we find ourselves living in an open historical moment; not simply a time of evolution or an age of revolution, but an extensive period of radical loss and surprising discovery as well. To the awakened eye, the world is seen as a living text that continues to unfold and be revealed in the dark times as well as in the brighter days. The world becomes what it has always been: a living mythos, an all-encompassing and unending story that holds everyone enthralled.

II

The SEARCH *for* MEANING *and* TRUTH

CHAPTER 6

GETTING TO THE
BOTTOM OF THINGS

*Liberation happens each time we become conscious
of the contents of the soul.*

Descent is the way of the soul from the beginning. We are the descendants of all who came before us, and the inheritors of the timeless treasury of the soul. We fall into the world by virtue of a specific inner gravity that would have us continue to grow deeper and at the same time, grow up. Thus, the struggle to develop and grow, to become our true selves must involve descent as well as ascent. As old alchemical ideas had it, upward movement eternalizes while downward movement personalizes. Spirit may call us to awaken to a greater sense of self; soul would have us connect more deeply to the ground of being. To the soul, down and back can be the same thing. Growing *down* can lead to awakening root memories that are inherited and can awaken and shape our lives from within and below.

The old notion of a dark night of the soul carries the ancient intuition that when something essential is missing, we must search for it in the depths of our soul. Whether we choose it or not, once a descent begins, we must not simply survive, but bring something back from the dark night of the soul that is missing or lacking in the world above—not something tangible such as an invention, but rather knowledge that can change life from within. Such knowledge used to be known as inner truth, the kind of truth hidden within us as well as within the world all around us. Another name for the kind of knowing that combines an awareness of that which is dark and that which is light is "dark knowledge."

When I was first sentenced to solitary confinement in a military prison I had no idea what manner of dark knowledge I might experience. However, there were immediate hints of what might come. There was another prisoner in a cell near mine. He was younger than me, only nineteen-years-old. At first, I was glad he was there. It was comforting to have some company nearby, even though we couldn't see each other. If we stood at the front bars of our cells, we could speak and hear each other. After a while, it became clear that he was deeply disturbed and easily agitated. Though I was a sympathetic neighbor, I knew instinctively that he needed more help than I could offer.

He told me that he, too, was in prison for refusing to obey orders, although he was vague about the circumstances, and what he had been ordered to do. Meanwhile, he said he had a good plan and expected to be free soon. He revealed to me that he had swallowed a handful of nuts and bolts with the expectation that the military would have to remove them for his own safety. After that, he felt sure they would deem him unfit for service and send him home. It did not occur to him that the authorities might take their time, even drag their feet on the whole issue, while he suffered severe internal pain, both physical and mental.

During the daytime, he would constantly ask the guards when he would be taken for X-rays and receive treatment. At night, he would often scream in pain and yell incoherently. When the guards came to quiet him, he would curse and provoke them until they stormed his cell. They would grapple with him until he tired of the struggle. Only after they subdued him would he settle down and finally become quiet.

As time wore on, he became more agitated and on edge and the guards, in turn, became more reactive and brutal. Despite his irrational and self-destructive behavior, the guards believed that he was intentionally trying to frustrate them while he tried to trick his way out of the army. I tried to explain to them that he was suffering from genuine emotional issues and likely a mental disorder as well. That meant little to them as most thought he deserved whatever happened for not straightening up and simply doing his duty. It was hard to believe that they could not see or somehow feel what, to me, were clear signs of genuine emotional and mental problems. Even the captain of the prison seemed to accept that the nightly battles would simply continue until some higher authority settled the matter.

The poor guy was very excited when they finally took him to the hospital to have surgery in order to remove the hardware from his stomach. I wished him well, but inside myself I worried about what might happen to him. I was deeply saddened when the guards later told me of his twisted fate. After he recovered from surgery, he was to be sent directly back to his company in order to serve out his time in the military. Not only that; but the cost of the operation and the expenses of his hospital stay would be regularly deducted from his pay.

A PHILOSOPHICAL PROBLEM

As time went on, my own talks with the captain made it clear that the higher authorities believed I would eventually give in and agree to become an obedient soldier. The guards continued to give me orders despite the fact that I refused to follow any. I would point out the rather obvious fact that I was already in solitary confinement and had lost all privileges. Meanwhile, I began learning to concentrate my thoughts while also developing a routine of calisthenics. I was instinctively trying to keep myself mentally and physically steady. Ironically, I found myself using exercises I had learned in military training to keep fit as I struggled to figure how to get out of the army.

Weeks went by and when I did not seem to falter in any way, a new campaign was undertaken, which was intended to break my will. It seemed to be a kind of carrot and stick strategy. On some days, an officer would arrive and offer me an immediate release from prison if I would agree to simply return to my regiment. On other days, I would be warned that a plan was underway to send me to a federal prison for many years.

Eventually, it dawned on me that it was not simply that we had reached a deadlock with regard to my position of not following orders. In addition to that there was a philosophical misunderstanding. No matter how I acted, no matter what I said, I still looked like a soldier to them. Since I resided in a military stockade, continued to wear a uniform, and ate army meals, I must, in fact, be a member of the military. If I was in the military, it followed that I had to obey the rules and follow orders. I realized that if I continued to look like a soldier, they would continue to expect me to act like one.

When evening came, I took off my uniform and threw it into the hallway along with all the bedding and army blankets. It seems strange now, but in the extremity of the situation, it made sense at the time. I had been told over and over that in signing the induction papers and entering the army, I had given up all my rights as a citizen. Now, I stood almost naked behind the bars of my cell, with nothing other than a metal bunk suspended from the cinder block walls. By having nothing in the cell with me that belonged to the military, I tried to demonstrate that I did not belong there. What came as a surprise to me was the distinct feeling in my bones that I was not there.

It was not simply that I was absent from duty, more that I was not present in the sense that they thought I should be. I had not lost touch with reality. I knew I was in a military prison; but I had also come to know that inside the walls of my soul, the battle was over. To them, I still appeared to be someone who could be intimidated or somehow forced to give up what they believed was simply a self-serving strategy. Inside myself, although I could feel sudden waves of loneliness, I had begun to settle on what felt like the bare ground of my being.

FASTING AGAINST THEM

The morning after I threw out my clothes and bedding from my cell, the guards threw them back in and ordered me to dress before breakfast. I calmly threw the clothes back out. They returned with a breakfast tray and wanted to exchange it for me putting the uniform back on. I liked breakfast; partly because in prison it could be a halfway decent meal. I also liked the sense of an almost normal beginning for what would inevitably become another long day in confinement. However, I continued to refuse to put on the uniform. Eventually, they pushed the breakfast tray inside the cell anyway.

I looked at the tray just inside the cell bars for a long time. Despite the allure of food, it dawned on me that if I began to eat, there would be a glaring fault in my new position. If I ate army food, it would still appear that I was present and participating as a member of the military. If I was part of the military I was, willingly or not, subject to the cycle of orders and punishment. I pushed the tray back into the hallway, where it sat for hours. For days afterward, the guards continued to bring trays of food several times a day, leaving them inside the cell in order to tempt me to eat. Not fully understanding what was driving me and having no idea how long I might be able to go without food, I told myself that I would decide each day whether to eat or continue fasting.

Deciding not to eat did not simply affect me body and soul, it seemed to change everything. When I refused to accept food it seemed as if the guards were personally offended. There was a vague sense that some level of shared humanity was being rejected and they were somehow affected as well. As I began to feel the early effects of fasting, I also began to realize that even the smallest semblance of a civilized exchange between me and the guards had come to an end.

After many weeks without food, I became not only visibly thin, but somewhat fragile. Then one day, I was wrapped in blankets and quietly moved out of the stockade. I was told I was being taken to a hospital and felt confused when I found myself in another solitary cell. It turned out that both things were true: my new place of confinement was a dark cell at the back of Gorgas Hospital. The hospital had been built for treating workers during the construction of the Panama Canal. Apparently, a block of prison cells had also been constructed. Hardly anyone knew that those cells even existed as they had not been used for decades. When I was informed that I was the only prisoner who had been in that cell for many decades, I thought of my troubled young friend from the solitary cells in the stockade. I wondered how I would be made to pay for my own visit to a hospital.

The cell was eerily quiet and I don't recall there being any windows. But, there were no bars either and there was an actual bed which even I would acknowledge I needed. I do recall being thoroughly examined by a series of doctors trying to determine what the effect of over a month of fasting was having on my health. During the testing I learned that it is impossible to predict how long a particular person can live without food. The capacity to survive starvation varies greatly depending upon individual genetics and health history, but can also be affected by isolation and other psychological factors.

There I was, the only prisoner in an otherwise unused prison. Although I had very little strength, there was an armed soldier standing guard outside the door, day and night. Not that they thought I might jump out of bed and try to escape; I was in no shape for that. Military rules required that a guard had to be present at all times. The regulations also required that the guards had to come from my original company, which turned out to be a good thing. Many of them were draftees like me, and most were sympathetic to my situation. Instead of receiving endless orders and threats from prison guards, I could actually have meaningful conversations and receive news of the outside world.

Part of the news the soldiers from my company conveyed to me was that everyone involved in the military knew about the fast I had undertaken. There were even reporters from newspapers and magazines from back in the states snooping around and asking questions. As certain guards described it, there was an increasing sense that I might suddenly die, and that would be big news. According to them, the authorities had first feared that if I managed to protest my way out of service, other draftees might try the same thing. That would create a great scandal with unpredictable consequences. Increasingly, however, the fear became that if I died of starvation there would be an even greater scandal.

Meanwhile, I would be regularly awakened in the night by doctors who would come over from the hospital to examine me. They would wake me to say that they could not find my pulse or detect the common signs of life. Often, they would ask if I really wanted to die. The question seemed more like a challenge than a voicing of concern. At times it even seemed to be an accusation, as if they wanted to wash their hands of any potential guilt or responsibility beforehand. If I died on their watch, it had to be the result of a death wish on my part, not because of any negligence or failure on their part.

I would answer that I did not wish to die; that dying was not the point as much as making clear how I wanted to live. They had great trouble understanding me and truthfully, I was still having trouble understanding myself. I had refused to go to war and possibly die under terms I could not agree with, only to enter a life-threatening battle of my own. I became literally caught between life and death, as it seemed that in order to understand myself; I had to face death in my own way. At some point during those long, empty nights, I did make my peace with death. It was certainly not that I wanted to die, but rather that I had found enough pieces of myself to feel some sense of being at peace with myself.

Meanwhile, the company guards who took turns at the door would often make a point of telling me that they did not want me to die. At the same time, the officers who continued to visit me seemed more uncertain where to lay the blame or the guilt for what everyone feared was about to happen. Some were genuinely sympathetic and wanted me to know that they did not agree with the official plan. Those who were unsympathetic would insist that there was no way that the American military was going to allow a negligent soldier to leave the army on their own terms. In the midst of the controversy and concern, I became suspended in time, floating somewhere between the living and the dead.

FORCE FEEDING

As it became clear that something needed to be done, an older military doctor arrived all the way from Washington D.C. I was told that he had actual experience with the effects of starvation because he helped survivors of the Nazi death camps during the war in Europe. He was different than the other doctors as he carefully explained how starvation worked and what lasting damage could be done to my organs even if I survived the fast. He repeated with greater authority that no one could predict what damage had already been done or at what point I might suddenly die. I don't know what role, if any, he played in what happened next.

One morning, a military doctor and some unfamiliar soldiers came into the cell and told me to sit at the side of the bed. They may have explained the procedure that was to follow, but I don't recall any of it if they did. As two soldiers held my arms at each side, the doctor placed a clamp against my lips. As I tried to keep my mouth closed, the clamp slowly forced my teeth open. Then, a plunger was used to force food into my mouth and down my throat. Although it was more of a liquid than solid food, the process immediately made my throat raw. Because it was ice-cold it felt more like a blow to the stomach than a delivery of nourishment.

After the initial shock, the process of force-feeding was repeated twice a day. I soon stopped physically resisting because it only made things more painful for me and for the guards, who would have to use force each time I resisted. Although I never agreed to the process, the effect of the regimen of force-feeding was that it forced me to remain alive. Every day I gained a little strength, although each application of the antiquated instruments of force made me feel as though I had moved from an old unused prison in Panama to a dungeon in medieval times.

Certainly, the dial had moved more toward the direction of life than death, but everyone agreed that we were in uncharted territory, not only in regard to my health but how we might resolve the situation. When there came a day during which no one appeared to administer a force-feeding, I went right back to fasting. After what seemed to be a final test, efforts were quietly put toward finding a process through which I might be discharged. Although there was much confusion and additional mistreatment, those in charge eventually found a way to issue a discharge without the further attention that would be caused by a general court martial.

Because I had been in various states of suspended animation during that period, details remained blurred in my memory. At times, there seemed to be no difference between night and day, and at times I didn't know if I was dead or in another world. Some things, however, still stand out quite clearly. I frequently recall the warning of the older doctor that I might already have suffered internal organ damage. And, I remember the doctors who examined me, before the force-feeding, and how they would begin by saying that I weighed just 87 pounds. Since I had entered the army at about 150 pounds, I had lost more than one-third of my body weight in less than two months.

Those details seemed to be mostly aspects of an unusual personal experience, until years later when I happened to read news reports from a prison in Ireland. The stories were about prisoners going on extensive hunger strikes to protest mistreatment at a

British prison camp in Northern Ireland. In the course of fighting for their rights as political prisoners, ten members of what became known as the "H-Block hunger strikers" had died of starvation while in custody. Most had died while being kept in solitary cells. Amongst them was Bobby Sands, an elected Member of the British Parliament, who would become known in poetry and song for fasting against the misuse of authority.

The details concerning the length of time that the prisoners fasted and how long they were able to last without any nourishment got my attention. Since both sides of my family originated in Ireland, I also felt an immediate connection to the painful history of protesting against colonial injustice. However, I was stunned to read that, when denied their rights and feeling unjustly treated, the prisoners had enacted an old Irish tradition of ritual fasting. The article did not give a name to the ritual practice or describe its origins; it simply stated that such a practice existed in ancient times. All of a sudden I understood that my decision to fast while in prison was not simply personal. It was also part of an ancestral tradition that, under pressure, had awakened, as if from inside my bones, and from the depths of my soul. To me, that seemed to confirm a surprising revelation of a dark knowledge that I had learned in my own solitary confinement, while in the dark night of my own soul.

JUSTICE AND THE SOUL

Research into ancient Irish practices eventually led me to an old code of honor known as the Brehon Laws. Under this code, a person could fast against anyone of a higher rank or holding a position of power who had injured them in some way. The ancient practice sought to empower an individual who felt the need to bring a person or party in a more dominant position to justice. If a person had a claim of injustice against someone of a higher rank, they could undertake a public ritual of fasting in order to force a genuine hearing of the facts and circumstances. This sanctioned form of public protest was called *troscad*, or ritual fasting. *Troscad* can be roughly translated as "fasting on or against a person" or "achieving justice by starvation."

The person initiating the ritual protest would sit before the door of the more powerful person and remain without food until arbitration or an administration of justice occurred. By fasting on the threshold of a house or an institution, a person not only brought attention to an injustice, but also might bring a kind of misfortune called "soul pollution" upon their oppressor. There was also a spiritual penalty to pay as there was such a great social and moral regard for hospitality among the Irish people, which extended even to strangers at one's door. To allow someone to starve to death at one's doorstep would be a profound disgrace and an indication of a lack of genuine soul.

The more powerful party could not simply ignore the protest, nor could they simply use force to stop it. If the accused party ignored the appeal to justice, they would themselves lose the protection and the benefits of the law. Ignoring a just claim of a soul injury would eventually cause harm to the soul of the accused person. At the same time the imbalance of power was shown to be a danger to the entire community. A misuse of position or power could cause a "soul injury" that had to be addressed or there could be no shared sense of justice and no trust in those who held the positions of authority.

However, if those being fasted against could admit some responsibility and offer some redress, the ritual of fasting would stop and social harmony would be restored. Because the results of fasting could be so damaging to the person seeking to correct an injustice, the ritual of fasting would not be entered lightly, but with full knowledge of the seriousness of the final result. At the same time, because the ancient understanding of humanity included the sense that each soul was secretly connected to the world soul, serious practices like fasting for justice could be seen to affect not only the "community of souls," but also the world.

The practice of ritual fasting was seen as a way of "shaping the world" by realigning the human community with the underlying Soul of the World. If injustice was allowed to go unchallenged and be sanctified by those in authority, it could only grow and lead to a greater imbalance of power and loss of soul at a collective level. If the sense that each individual soul had inner worth and innate nobility became lost, then the entire community could lose all sense of genuine meaning and the world could begin to fall out of balance. The desire to eat and survive is instinctive and essential to humanity; the need for truth and justice is another kind of nourishment that can run as deep as the soul.

THE FORCE OF TRUTH

One of the most notable modern occasions of ritual fasting involved the mayor of the city of Cork in Ireland. In 1920, he was arrested by the British administration after refusing to recognize the authority of a military tribunal. He argued that the tribunal had no right to pass judgment against someone properly acting on behalf of a city and its people. Subsequently, he was forcibly removed from Ireland and placed in a London prison, where he died on the seventy-fourth day of his ritual fast against injustice.

News reports that spread across the world included descriptions of the ancient tradition of fasting against unjust uses of power and authority. Those reports and the story of the sacrifice of the mayor are said to have reached Mahatma Gandhi, who was fighting against colonial injustice in India. Gandhi recognized that the Irish tradition of ritual fasting had strong similarities to an ancient custom in India called *acharitan*. Eventually, he revived the ancient practice of fasting and used it as part of a moral political force against the colonial rule under which the people of India had suffered for many years.

Ancient Irish words for justice include the idea of being "in accord with the truth," especially the sense that a deep and even cosmic level of truth resides at the bottom of things. Gandhi also drew upon the deeper understanding of the meanings of both truth and justice that can be found in ancient traditions in India. He named his stand against corrupt power and social injustice *satyagraha*, which translates as "insistence on truth," or "the force of truth." *Satya* is a deep word that can mean "truth in speech;" but also implies love and beauty. This was critical to Gandhi's understanding of using nonviolent means in seeking for both truth and justice.

The core idea that underlies the ancient practices found in both Ireland and India is the sense that truth and justice are not simply legal or political concerns, but are essentially issues of the soul. As such, any search for truth and justice involves the community as well as the individual and it can affect the entire world as well.

We are the descendants of all who came before us and the beneficiaries of all who suffered and struggled for truth and justice in their own times and in their own ways. Even if the old practices have fallen out of conscious use, they wait nearby for us to descend and find the intelligence and meanings of them again. Many ancient traditions imagined that the world had a living soul and that the bedrock underlying the world as well as each person alive in it was something similar to satya—the ground of truth and beauty that might be forgotten, but that can never be destroyed. When truth is being denied, when justice seems lost, we must descend to the depths of the soul and the ground of being to find their living roots again. In the dark times we must find the kind of wisdom that combines an understanding of the darkness and the light.

CHAPTER 7

THE FORGOTTEN STORY

The whole world trembles on the edge of revealing
its own immanent soul.

The tattered text of the World Weary Man arguing with his Ba-soul has not only stood the test of time, it reminds us that something timeless is set within each of us. More than a footnote in history or an oddity of scholarship, it represents a collective memory as well as an individual calling to awaken to the natural inheritance of the soul. Though we are born into history and must suffer the times we live in, the story of the soul is timeless and rooted in things eternal. It has always been a part of human nature and an aspect of the human dilemma to participate in both worlds. We live in more than one world and thus need more than one kind of knowledge to survive.

Upon being released from prison, I knew I had found a distinct connection to my own soul. Yet, like the incomplete story of the World Weary Man, it was not clear how things might turn out. In the isolation of the solitary cell, I experienced a revelation of something meaningful inside myself that I barely knew that somehow seemed to know me well. Since I had found that sense of presence after feeling I had lost everything and hit bottom, I imagined it as the "underlying soul." In one sense, I meant that it was underlying everything I knew and everything I did with my life. In another way, I meant that it had been hidden underneath the lies I would tell myself in order to avoid facing feelings of uncertainty and fears of being empty inside.

When I returned to the daily world, I felt exhausted, but not empty. I felt altered, but unclear how to understand what I had gone through. I had great difficulty explaining what had happened and soon learned that most people did not or could not hear it anyway. Like many others who undergo life-changing events, I had trouble finding people who would listen to what I could not fully understand, yet had to talk about. Though I had a story to tell, I was far from being able to tell it, much less understand it myself. Like many who survive a war, a natural disaster, or a tragic loss, a level of turbulence and trauma continued unabated within me.

At issue was not only an inability to fit back into daily life, but also the feeling that while I had survived, something had died. It was not only that I was in a post-traumatic condition, but also that I had become a different person and felt like a stranger in a strange land. Rather than recovering a sense of normal life, I was in danger of feeling as lost in the outer world as I had been at times while locked inside the prison. Not knowing exactly how to pick up the threads of life, I began to study death. Not simply the notion of mortality and the end of life, but also death as something we can unexpectedly brush against in the course of life.

A LITTLE DEATH, A GREATER LIFE

I read what poets and philosophers had to say about death and dying. I also collected proverbs and stories from ancient traditions that saw death quite differently than in modern culture. Whereas most people in the modern world consider death to simply be the grim opposite of life, ancient people considered death to be a part of life ongoing. Birth and death could be seen as opposite poles, and the great arc of life included both of them. The sense that a new stage of life can grow out of the death of the previous phase was common knowledge to those living close to the natural cycles of life and death. Each phase of life could be seen to exhaust itself as something new or renewing tries to arise.

Yet, like the presence of an underlying soul, something about the place and meaning of death seems to have been lost on the way to modern life. "Death is the middle of a long life," an old Irish proverb puts it succinctly. In such a conception, death appears not just at the end, but also right in the middle of things. Thus, knowing something about the nature of death could lead to knowing more about the essence and meaning of life.

The modern tendency to literalize death makes the nature of genuine change and transformation more difficult to imagine and approach. "Little death" is a useful term that can be used to draw a distinction between the end of a life and the kind of transformation that can happen and be needed in the course of life. When seen in the middle of the trilogy of life-death-rebirth, death becomes not simply the final act, but also a critical step in each transition to a life of greater meaning and deeper understanding.

Transformation was once considered to be the fundamental law and core dynamic of the soul. The problem is that in order to find a new form, the old formation or formulation must die. The word *transform* means to "undergo a change of form;" to change not the appearance, but the very form of one's existence. If we can suffer a little death, the next version of our life can be born. Life and death can thus be found to be secretly conspiring to make rebirth or renewal possible.

In human life, the old formation tends to be the shape of a person's ego or "little-self." The problem is that the little-self typically does not know and will not trust that there is a deeper self within that knows the true shape and aim of our life. The idea of a little-death generating a greater sense of self leads directly to the age-old problem of the little-self as the faulty and insecure ruler of our lives. As Plato once said, "Be kind, for everyone you meet is fighting a hard battle." He was referring to the battle between the little-self that tries to control life and the greater self or deeper soul within us, which knows exactly how our lives are intended to be.

THE MYTH OF ER

It was also Plato who recounted a mythical tale about how each soul has a unique shape and distinct destiny, despite most people failing to awaken to that knowledge. The ancient narrative includes a profound vision of the birth of the human soul and a radical experience of death and rebirth as well. The story is called the Myth of Er, a name that echoes the sense of common "earth." Very little is told of the origins or history of Er and nothing is said about his later life. Similar to the World Weary Man, Er serves as a kind of everyman or representative of every person who suffers life on earth.

Plato states right at the beginning that this is not an epic story involving one of the great heroes of the ancient world. Rather, it is an unusual report of someone who happened to fall in combat and was left for dead on the battlefield. Since nothing much is said about the war and little information offered about the battle, it could be any war or any battle at all.

The tale begins when Er has already fallen on the battlefield, where he languished for days beneath a pile of corpses. Somehow, his body remained uncorrupted and when he awoke, he found himself in a completely unfamiliar territory. When he saw a company of souls, he joined the group for what became a surprising and revealing journey through the underworld. In the course of things, Er was instructed to observe all that happened carefully in order that he might carry back to the living everything that he witnessed and learned while in the land of the dead.

One of the first things Er observed was a place where recently deceased souls were being judged for having been just or unjust while on earth. After witnessing the separation of the just from the unjust, Er continued to travel with the group of souls who were on their way to be born on earth. Soon, they arrived at a place of surpassing vision and wonder. They appeared to be at the very center of the cosmos where they watched in amazement as a great spindle seemed to generate the revolutions and rotations of all the planets and the spheres. The spindle rested upon the knees of Ananke, described as the Goddess of Necessity, before whom even the gods must bow.

Sitting near the base of the cosmic spindle were the daughters of Necessity. Known as the three Sisters of Fate, they represent the past, present, and future and weave the fateful web of time and space that holds each soul in the cosmic net of life. As the sisters chanted along with the music of the spheres, they would by turn give the spindle a spin in order to keep the universe turning.

As Er watched in awe, a guide appeared who began preparing the souls to pass one by one before the three sisters, who would decide the fate of those souls about to be born on earth. The guide pointed out that they would not be assigned a fate, but that each would choose their own lot in life. Then he brought them before Lachesis, the first Sister of Fate and dispenser of lots. The guide then disclosed that as soon as they would choose their lot in life, they would also receive a genius, or inner guide of their own who would accompany them throughout their adventure on earth.

After each of the souls had chosen their lot, their guardian spirit would accompany them to Clotho, also known as "the spinner." From her we get the word "cloth" as well as "clothes" and other words related to spinning and weaving. As each soul appeared before her, Clotho would pull into existence the invisible thread of fate that would secretly run through each person's life. She would spin out the destiny and aim of each soul and at the last moment give each one about to be born a twist of fate that would make their life unique. Last of all, the guardian spirit brought each soul before Atropos, whose name means, "she who cannot be turned." Atropos would further pull the threads of their lives and make each lot and destiny irreversible. After being confirmed by her, they were all warned not to turn or look back as they now passed beneath the throne and the knee of Necessity.

After each had chosen the shape and aim of the life they would live on earth, the entire group crossed a desert-like area. After traveling for a time in the scorching heat, they found themselves at a strange place called the Plane of Forgetfulness. Toward evening, they encamped by a wide river that Er learned was called the River Lethe, but also known as the Stream of Forgetfulness. After settling by the banks of the streaming water, they were each obliged to drink a certain quantity. As soon as each one drank of the waters of oblivion, they completely forgot everything that had happened in the course of their underworld journey. All memory of being at the very center of the cosmos was washed away in a moment and any trace of the lot in life and the destiny they had chosen became completely forgotten.

Only Er was hindered from drinking the water of forgetfulness;

otherwise, the whole adventure would have been forgotten and there would be no tale to tell. Er stayed awake and alert as the others dropped into the sleep of forgetfulness and night fell on the Plane of Forgetfulness. During the middle of the night, there came a thunderstorm and an earthquake at the same time, as if both heaven and earth were signaling something important. In that eruptive moment the company of souls departed the Plane of Forgetfulness and were driven upwards, like shooting stars entering the world.

In all manner of ways and shapes they each arrived at the time and place of their birth. But, by what means Er managed to return to earth he could not say. Just as abruptly as he had previously awakened in the underworld, he awoke again and came back to life. And, it was none too soon as he found himself lying on a pyre at his own funeral.

The strange story of the journey to the underworld ends abruptly at a funeral that also seems to be a nativity. Life comes back from death and Er returns as both the messenger and the message. He is the messenger because he brings back knowledge about the origins of the soul; and he is the message because he represents the reawakening of the soul as if from death. After being left for dead, he returns from the underworld as a kind of mythic survivor and cosmic informant. He delivers his salient message from the otherworld and is never heard from again. Yet he remains, century after century, like the World Weary Man, a messenger of the origins of the individual soul and the hidden message brought to life by each person born on earth.

At issue is not whether we should *believe* such a tale. For, myths are not about believing; rather, they are vehicles for imagining. The point is not to believe in a literal underworld, but to connect to a profound sense of otherness that ever dwells near at hand and within us as well. The imagination of the underworld opens a deep territory of inner life where the hidden message of soul waits to be discovered and brought to life. Imagination is the natural power of the soul and the extraordinary faculty that makes each of us capable of conceiving the entire cosmos. Humans are natural cosmologists and the soul's natural horizon is the cosmos. Unfortunately, the modern world tends to become smaller and more horizontal as it loses the vertical dimension and the grounding depths that the awakened soul would bring to life.

Unlike fantasy, which leads away from life, imagination is the mythic key that can unlock the destiny rooted in one's individual fate. Imagination is the spark of the divine within us that can link mind and body, leading to both healing ideas and revelatory images. Nothing is real unless it first passes through the realm of imagination and then passes beneath the knee of Necessity.

Each soul born bears a message trying to be remembered by its host in order to be delivered to the world. Each life is a mystery trying to be revealed and the strange story of Er points at what the revelation is intended to be. Each soul gets to choose an essential imagination and core pattern that gives that life its unique inner shape as well as its true aim and ultimate destiny. Seen in this way, the purpose of life becomes the process of awakening the underlying soul and remembering why we each came to life to begin with. Once awakened, our souls can intuit the secret connection of each individual to the cosmos, or the Soul of the World. The awakened soul then becomes a conduit for further messages trying to enter the world in the form of inspirations, dreams and imaginings that make life more meaningful and more beautiful.

THE FORGOTTEN STORY

The prehistory of the soul is the forgotten story of the Western world that has come to think that all of life might be accidental and each person nothing but a chance occurrence. This mostly forgotten story tells how we forget our mythical, cosmological origins. It explains how it could be that we keep forgetting things that are essential to our sense of self and our understanding of our place in the world around us. Failures of imagination leave us disconnected from both the ground of the soul and the heart of the cosmos and that disconnect must over time lead to both a loss of soul and a decline of culture. As imagination declines, forgetfulness increases and eventually leaves us with a culture dominated by narrow-mindedness, hardening hearts, and hardened laws.

The story of Er depicts a visionary journey through the underworld, but also a visitation to the center of the cosmos. At the point where the souls pass before the Goddess of Necessity, they are also in proximity of the "axis mundi," or world axis. As the center of the universe, it is seen as an axis. As a place of origin, it is imagined as the "omphalos," or navel of life. Either way, the mythical suggestion is that each soul comes from the center of the cosmos; each has heard the music of the spheres and felt the turning as well as the tuning at the center of it all. Despite forgetting all that happened before we were born, we each remain cosmologically connected. An invisible umbilical thread connects us to the center of existence and the Soul of the World.

Since each soul was once present at the center and remains tied to the invisible threads of eternity, should we find the center of ourselves, we might also find our connection to the center of existence. Rather than being nothing but random visitors in an accidental universe, we are called to awaken to a soulful connection, not just to our own life, but also to the center of all life. For, the message brought back from the otherworld includes the depiction of each soul being born as a unique light that departs from the center of the cosmos and bursts into the world like a shooting star.

Humans are the only mythologists and the only cosmologists; we are always trying to find the story that makes sense of things and the cosmology that accounts for everything. Even modern astrophysicists and theorists are trying to find missing threads of the story that surrounds us. The problem is that most are looking for a logical explanation when the world remains a living mystery. Part of the mystery is that we are tied to the universal by virtue of what is unique within us. When we lose or forget that we are each unique and unrepeatable, we lose our natural connection to the origins of life at the center of the cosmos.

We are a microcosm of the macrocosmic design, and if we can remember what first brought us to life we can add presence and meaning to the world simply by living the life we chose before we were born. If not, we will have no choice but to become ever more forgetful of the precise things that are intended to keep us all connected to the center of life and the ongoing song of existence.

The human soul is both mythical and cosmological by nature, leaving us unable to stop trying to imagine the entire world, how it all began, how it might end, and what role we are intended to play within it all. On one level, we can easily feel that we are just a tiny speck in the vast universe; on another level, as dreamers and lovers, as storytellers and seekers we can intuit that we are tied to the center and capable of imagining how we might contribute to the ongoing creation of the world.

Of course, notions of a cosmological connection and a latent pattern of the soul cannot be proven in a laboratory, unless the laboratory can be seen as life itself. The felt sense of innate meaning and life purpose comes as an intuitive awakening, not as a logical deduction. The real laboratory for humanity has always been the totality of life with its compelling dreams, puzzling challenges, surprising inspirations, and intuitive understandings. The very nature of humanity places each of us in the midst of the eternal drama, each a unique experiment of nature itself. Life is the laboratory wherein we experiment with the possibility of awakening to who and what we already are in the depths of our souls and at the core of our being.

More than an ego, or a little-self, that simply reacts to circumstances, what waits to be discovered is a genuine sense of self and soul. When faced with real trouble, there is no formula that can save us; there is only the possibility of turning within to connect more deeply with something already present and able to alter the course of both individual and collective life. The experience of awakening more fully is what the human soul anticipates and expects whenever we feel ourselves to be in a situation of life or death. For, the soul knows that a brush with death or a visit to the underworld is needed, in order to turn the spindle of fate and aim us more truly at the destiny already woven within our souls.

THE PROBLEM OF FORGETTING

The intensification of worldwide troubles and fears can be seen as a cultural crisis, but it can also be approached as a crisis of imagination that reaches to a cosmological level. During times of crises and catastrophe, we must look beyond what we already think we know or what we like to believe. Amidst the rush of outer events and the flood of data and endless details, we can easily feel that we are buried under layers of information that not only cannot change our lives, but simply add to the burdens we carry.

At the same time, the dead weight of history can be felt more intensely as the end of an age seems to come closer all the time. Like our forbearer Er, we may need a great shock in order to awaken to the essential energies and imagination that we carry within but have long forgotten or even denied. Strangely, when the world around us seems about to collapse, the inner pattern of the soul is moving closer to the surface and trying to become known.

The habit of forgetting exactly what we need to know occurs on both collective and individual levels. At certain times, we are in need of a wake-up call that rouses us from the collective lethargy and forgetfulness that can be so common in modern life. The River Lethe flows strongly through contemporary culture as more and more people question whether life has lost all sense meaning and purpose. Increasingly, contemporary life seems to be organized to take us away from what our hearts truly desire and what our souls most deeply need. Despite and because of all kinds of technologies and inventive devises, the modern world often can seem more like the Plane of Forgetfulness.

Great disasters and impossible tasks can provoke hidden resources and help reveal the underlying wholeness and unity of life; but only if we are willing to suffer the tensions until a new level of understanding dawns on us. Inside all stuck situations there exists a creative vulnerability that can lead to a release of unexpected imagination and a flow of new ideas. Yet, our sense of life must first become overwhelmed and we must feel as though we're on the verge of oblivion; only then can the life-saving, world renewing energies be found.

The modern method seeks to reduce the size of our problems in order to deal with them in bits and pieces. The mythological method would have us face up to the enormity of life's issues in order to rise to the levels of imagination and creativity waiting to awaken in our souls. In mythic terms, life is a mystery trying to be revealed. Yet, like any great mystery, some big things that have been hidden and forgotten must be uncovered before the truth of the drama can appear.

THE MEANING OF TRUTH

Part of the human dilemma is that we have all, by necessity, drank from the River Lethe and thus suffer various levels of forgetfulness, carelessness, and oblivion. The problem, now and for all time, is that what we came to life to be, and what we desperately seek to find, remains concealed within us and forgotten. When time seems to be running out and everything appears to be falling apart, the timeless aspects of life are actually closer to the surface and waiting to be recalled by us. Something subtle and enduring about the world is trying to be remembered and be rediscovered, and it seems to take some big trouble for us to awaken to it.

Interestingly, the Greek word for "truth" takes its form from the Lethe, the River of Forgetfulness. Whereas *lethe* means "oblivion and forgetfulness," *aletheia* means "truth and not to forget," especially not to forget the core truths of life. In the old myths, Lethe was also known as the *Ameles Potamos*, or the River of Carelessness and Unmindfulness, as if to say that we do not know our own mind until we enter the inner-under-otherworld to uncover and recover that which our soul knew before birth. We will be careless about the gift of our lives and unmindful of the world around us unless we awaken to the nature of our underlying souls.

From lethe we also get "lethargy" and "lethal." Thus, forgetting that our soul has a distinct shape and aim in life can leave us lost in lethargy instead of being awakened and fully alive. It has become easier to be lethargic, lacking in purpose, and wind up sleepwalking through life. And, that can be lethal if we become part of the, now popular, "walking dead."

In the strange symmetry of the underworld, the boundary waters on the left-hand appear as the River Lethe, the stream of forgetfulness, and the right-hand waters flow as the River of Mnemosyne and the deep well of memory and inspiration. We get our word "memory" from Mnemosyne, who was also known as the mother of the Muses. The waters of Mnemosyne were also called the Well of Rejuvenation, which could produce the "wineless ecstasy of memory."

Those who drink the waters of Lethe forget who they are intended to be and where they come from. Those who drink of the waters of Mnemosyne awaken to the well of deep memory, the stream of origins able to bring renewal and rejuvenation at any age and at any time in life. This inner well holds the original water of life, the *aqua vitae*, the eternal fountain of youth that resides in the depths of the soul and at the center of the psyche. Part of what has been forgotten in the common oblivion of the modern world is the innate connection to the unseen source of great memory and endless inspiration.

Mnemosyne presents a much more comprehensive idea than our common sense of memory. She is an active agent of the Cosmos imagined as a living being having the all-encompassing memory of the whole. As the archetype of Great Memory, she is in touch with the sacred memory of the source and all that is original and inspired in this world. Mnemosyne also gives birth to the Muses who bring both archetypal memory and potent inspirations to the minds and hearts of humankind.

The soul, or deep self, unerringly remembers what we keep forgetting. Yet, the little-self automatically wakes each morning thinking that it knows what to do and where to go. The ego keeps forgetting that it drank from the stream of forgetfulness and does not truly know what to do in life. Meanwhile, the deeper self does not forget and keeps trying to lead us down and back to the well of memory, the stream of truth hidden within the soul.

Each life has an inner truth that was sealed at birth and concealed in the depths of the soul. This inner truth is also the latent code of the soul that tries to become revealed in the course of our lives. *Alethia* means not to forget, to remember what is true. What is most true for each of us is the core pattern that first brought us to the door of life. Our core task and true life journey involve recollecting and remembering parts of ourselves that have been repressed or forgotten.

When a situation begins to feel like a matter of "life and death," the underlying soul is actually close at hand and trying to get our attention. Something in us is trying to die in order that a greater sense of self and soul might be born and grow. Thus, the troubles we find ourselves in are intended to wake us up to a greater sense of life and awaken the underlying soul, which knows better than us what our life is for. When seen from the deeper view of the soul, the challenges and obstacles in life are not simply roadblocks, intended to stop us altogether, as much as detours intended to lead us to genuine change and growth.

Life scrapes at us from the outside and the thread of our destiny pulls at us from within as both forces try to loosen the grip of the little-self in order that we might awaken to a greater sense and shape of life trying to be born from within. The gestation period for this kind of rebirth can be as long as it takes for us to realize, while wishing to embrace life more fully, that we are carrying a corpse. Our inner world must become overwhelmed and almost destroyed; only then can the life-saving, world-renewing energies be found. At both the collective and the individual levels, a meaningful path must involve little deaths if a greater life is to occur.

Life requires that we live through the troubles of our time in order to learn the deeper design that we carry within, one that can carry us where we truly need to go. For, culture is made and remade in the space between the individual and the collective. The opposite of nihilistic attitudes that result from a great forgetfulness cannot be something indefinite; it must be something of a different order. Ultimately, what stands against obliviousness and nihilism is the awakened individual. In times of great danger and oblivion it is the totality of a person and the deepest ideals of humanity that must be recalled and be served again.

The human soul has a mythic propensity and cosmological instinct for making something out of nothing. We are being asked to participate creatively in the changes sweeping through the world. In the great drama of life, the awakened human soul becomes the extra quantity and uniquely living quality needed to help tip the balance of the world away from destruction and toward ongoing creation. The counterbalance to collective forms of terror and destruction is found in individuals awakening to the underlying wholeness of the self and the secret connection of each to the soul of the world.

The old soul that dwells at the core of each person has a tolerance for chaos and an instinct for survival. Not in the simple biological terms of survival of the fittest, but a complex involvement with hidden aspects of creation. We can only come to know our soul when the chips are down, when there's nothing else to do but take on a bigger imagination of the cosmos and of our place within it. The return of cosmic order and cosmic sense always happens at the edge of the abyss, on the brink of disaster where life and beauty and meaning are snatched once again from the teeth of chaos.

There comes a time when we must allow something timeless to touch us in order to truly change and move beyond our fixed attitudes and limited understanding of the mysteries of life. When it seems like all might end in disaster, it becomes a question of finding the deeper imagination of life, the enduring patterns and essential stories that reunite us to the pulse of nature and the heart of culture. In the extremities of life and in times of loss, we can rediscover what is essentially ours, what cannot be taken from us unless we give up on our true self and soul.

CHAPTER 8

THE SOUL'S GREAT ADVENTURE

*Typically, our perceived realities make up only
a small part of the whole.*

Fire and heat were the essence at the origin of the universe. In modern thought, the world began with a singular event born of heat and density, now commonly called the Big Bang. Current theories about the earth's molten core compare its temperature to the fiery surface of the sun. Each day, the combustion of the sun continues to warm, if not overheat, the earth's surface, while a hidden inferno burns at the core of the planet that we call our home.

The world is on fire, much as Heraclitus described it 2500 years ago when he proclaimed the flame of life to be the first principle and the cosmos to be "an ever-living fire." Fire appears at the beginning and hides at the center of all that exists as "all things are exchanged for fire and fire for all things." Fire is both the physical incarnation of the constant heat of creation and the perpetual flux and flickering change at the heart of life.

All of life is on fire—a universal agony and ecstasy of burning, a living, breathing inspiration and illumination amidst the eternal sea of darkness. Under the old adage of "as above so below," we are also on fire; we who are born of this cosmic heat and constant flux are burning as well. Most people sustain a body heat of ninety-eight degrees, give or take a bit, regardless of the outside temperature. To live on earth means to burn one way or another. What we call our life is also a form of combustion. We heat up with passions and become "all fired up" with ideas. We "carry a flame" for those we love and at times burn life's candle at both ends. We are on fire, each soul a spark of creation, a star falling from the eternal sky to the dark earth.

There is a fire at the center of the earth and a flame at the center of our hearts. The divine spark within us is the gift of life, a burning birthright that makes us both the children of, and at times the agents of, ongoing creation. We share in the illumination of stars, in the burning heat of animals, and ever more subtly in the cooler green fire of trees and the blue-black smoldering of the waters. Our inner spark burns with varying intensity throughout life and many imagine that its embers last beyond the moment when death separates the body and soul.

The flame that burns within us is our inner nature seen in its fiery form. Because it can take many forms, the inner spark goes by many names: spirit, imagination, purpose, intelligence, consciousness; soul, wisdom, genius, daimon and even demon. The spark of life generates both heat and light. It burns with the heat of "libido," the vital life energy that makes us warm-blooded and prone to feverish passions. Yet, the inner spark can become more illumination than heat if, and when, it burns in the right direction. The divine spark is both the living seed of our life potential and the inner light of the soul.

THE TWO ARCS OF LIFE

Because we are complex and sometimes conscious beings, our life project involves more than one arc of existence and more than the single aim of survival. We must make our way in the world as we find it, and we are also intended to awaken to the way of being already planted within us as a divine spark-seed. We must wander through the world and struggle with our fate in order to find again the specific spark of life which was given to us to begin with.

An old idea, still remembered in India, describes the essential spark of life as burning along two distinct arcs. The First Arc of Life begins with the first breath we take as part of the course of human development that leads to "growing up" and entering the outer world. This is the growth curve that leads to various careers in life and often to growing one's own family. While following the first arc we "make a life" and learn to make our way in the day-to-day world.

The Second Arc of Life turns inward to illuminate the path of awakening and the work of growing more soul from the original seed set within us. The second arc concerns the inner life of self-reflection and the hidden spark of spiritual growth. This second arc is not dependent on contemporary circumstances as much as engendered by something original and unique to our lives. In following this inner arc, we grow deeper within ourselves and learn the shape and aim of our true nature.

Unless interrupted, the curve of time carries a person from childhood to youth, from youth to adult, from adult to old age. Much of this happens as a matter of course, for it is the natural course and curve of growth in human life. Growing up, becoming independent, and finding a way to live in common society are all essential aspects of the initial arc. They are also primary challenges for the individual ego, or little-self, as we seek to find ways to fit in and establish ourselves in daily life.

While both arcs are ignited by the original spark in one's soul, the outward arc takes precedence early on as we establish our place in the world. This outward arc is characterized by self-assertion as each person undertakes social responsibilities and pursues outer aims. In old traditions, the first arc has been called the Arc of Self-Assertion, the Path of Pursuit, the Road of Attainment, and when seen collectively, the Evolutionary Curve.

The second arc of life involves an involution or turning within to seek self-knowledge and develop greater self-awareness. This inward arc depends upon reflection, remembering, and becoming aware of the core pattern of one's soul and the inherent purpose of one's life. The inner arc bends toward things eternal; it involves the dream of one's life as well as the life of one's dreams. This is the arc of growing consciousness, genuine calling, and potentially of spiritual fulfillment. The second arc of life has been described as the Interior Road, the Path of Return, the Arc of Realization, and the Path of Surrender.

The outer arc depends upon direct action and explicit goals; it involves growing up, stepping out, and finding some sense of standing within collective life. The second arc focuses upon awakening within and growing deeper instead of simply growing up. It can also require slowing down instead of rushing along with the mainstream of life. First a person must grow up and "get a life;" after that they must grow within in order to make their life have meaning. First, make a full life, then seek and search for some fulfillment within that life.

If the first arc has to do with basic needs and common wants, the project of the second arc has more to do with the great longings and deep desires that inhabit the soul. The second arc involves eternal things instead of external things. Here, the inner spark burns toward transcendence of the common world in favor of the inner project of the soul; in that sense, it is not dependent on contemporary circumstances as much as engendered by something ancient and knowing within us.

Often the two arcs are considered in terms of the two halves of life. Typically, the first arc tends to dominate early in life as it involves achieving practical goals and dealing with the "hard facts of life." Later in life, the inner arc tries to surface more and lead away from the pressures and distractions of the daily world. As an "arc of release," it involves a process of "letting go" of those things most people strive to attain through the arc of achievement. Instead of seeking greater wealth or higher social status, a person turns to the work of growing the soul and seeking spiritual fulfillment.

In actual experience, the inner and outer arcs can intersect and interact throughout a person's life. Each soul is by nature unique and in each life project the two arcs can overlap and alternate in complex ways. At a given time, our energy for growth and change can be either more inwardly inclined or more outward bound.

In modern Western societies, the inner arc is often undervalued, certainly less understood, and at times even ignored. Mass cultures that focus on material goods, technical achievements, and practical knowledge can have little interest in the individual soul with its hidden longings and expectations for genuine transformation. Typically, accomplishments must be measurable and all too often, the outer world remains the only focal point throughout life.

One consequence of this outward focus is that the dilemma of who we are supposed to be in the world is solved in too narrow a way. We limit ourselves to common expectations and attainable goals, and this leads to the loss of inner resources and natural propensities of the soul. Many people simply "grow old" and die without awakening to the nature of the divine seed hidden within them. Instead of slowing down and growing inward, many remain focused upon outer issues, material attainments, and the opinions of others. The resulting lack of insight into life and paucity of inner growth tends to make the later stages of life seem more about failure and loss than about spiritual fulfillment and release.

Seen from the view of hard reality, the issues of the second arc can seem unreal, not just wrong-headed, but also foolish. However, when the concerns of our ego and the habits developed in the first arc continue to dominate our awareness, life can "lose its spark" and seem to have no real point. The original spark of our lives must occasionally be rekindled by a radical shift of attention or the experience of an altered state. Some touch of the eternal spark of love and life must be found, and some vital elements of the soul must at least temporarily awaken or else everything can seem empty and meaningless.

Whether we recognize it or not, when our energy drains from life's outer projects, our attention is being drawn inward, downward and back towards the original spark of our lives and the genuine project of our soul. The little-self must be set aside long enough for the light of the second arc to shine through and illuminate a genuine life-path. Although surprising when we find it, the path of the soul turns out to have been ingrained within us, a part of us all along. At critical turning points in life, even a great disappointment can be a message to reorient ourselves to something set within us to begin with.

LADDERS OF LIFE

An old parable depicts the dilemma that can develop when the arc of self-assertion and attainment dominates a person's life. The story tells of a man who happened to come upon a tall ladder leaning against a high wall. He took the appearance of the ladder as a challenge to climb all the way to the top of the wall. He wanted to reach the peak and see what it felt like to be on top of it all. Putting all else aside, he began to climb and continued rising rung after rung until he reached the pinnacle. Only after attaining that height was he able to see that the ladder was leaning against the wrong wall.

Higher and higher he had risen, all the while imagining the fulfillment of reaching the top and achieving a great goal. Instead, he found himself at the height of disappointment because his soul was secretly aimed another way. Only on the way back down did he begin to consider that his life might have been pointed at something different all along. That secondary recognition and the reflections it can generate about life become the ground from which the inner arc can begin to develop and the true aim of the soul become revealed.

The point of the story is not to avoid all the ladders or be absolutely sure to climb the right one. That would lead to avoiding the lessons of the first arc in order to succeed at the second one. The problem isn't that the instinct to climb is simply erroneous. We enter the world wherever we happen to be and learn to work our way out or climb our way up. Something has to be attempted. Human memory carries the sense of ascent from below and instinctively keeps climbing up from the mud of creation.

Life's first arc—and the continuance of the species—depend upon our willingness to throw ourselves into the fray and do our best with whatever walls and obstacles we might be facing. However, if the issues of our inner life and the deeper project of the soul are repeatedly put off in favor of the next rung on the ladder, then the fall can be devastating when it finally does come.

In the first arc of life, we climb the ladders that appear before us. We succeed or we fail; we rise to the top of the heap or keep slipping down and losing our way. The point of all the striving along the arc of attainment lies mostly in the effort that is given. Simply getting the "upper hand" doesn't mean becoming one's self in a genuine way. There's knowledge to be discovered at the bottom of the heap that is equal to what can be learned at the top. Seen from underneath, all the upward mobility of the world appears to be just a bit pretentious.

While ambition can be a natural and good thing, willful ambition—without a genuine connection to the orientation and longings of a person's soul—can lead to a dead end. Whether it appears in academic strivings of youth or in the competitive struggle of career-oriented people, unfettered and ungrounded ambition can lead to deep disorientation and alienation at the level of the soul.

Although the meaning of the word has become linked to overreaching desire and grouped with pride, vainglory, and arrogance, *ambition* comes from Latin roots meaning "a going around." Natural ambition means to learn the ambit or circumference of one's soul. In ancient times, people born to nobility might have to walk the ambit of their realm in order to know the scope and resources at their disposal.

However, the deeper sense of the ambit includes the idea that each soul, by virtue of being born has some nobility. Thus, natural ambition would involve becoming more conscious and aware of the scope and resources of one's inner realm. It was in that sense that young nobles as well as aboriginal youth would go on "walkabout" before taking on the burdens and responsibilities of daily life.

Meanwhile, the soul's great project begins where the little-self leaves off. For, the soul can find success in our worst failures, and find hints of failure in what others see as great success. Often the soul tries to awaken exactly where life disappoints us and this awakening can happen even when we reach what others consider to be the pinnacles of achievement. Inside the great disappointments with the first arc of life can be found the hidden appointment that the soul desired all along the way. For, the soul aspires to deeper things and inner goals whether we find success or failure in the daily world.

Along the arc of return, many things are seen differently and many events can be revalued. We can find soul in surprise and in failure, in anything that wakes us up more fully or pulls us down and deeper into life. The great challenge is to learn the unique way of one's soul and to keep making soul from both the gains and losses found in life. Along the arc where one returns to the core pattern of the soul, success and failure can be of equal interest. In the inevitable peaks and valleys of life we are intended to rise and fall repeatedly. In doing so we find the way we are aimed at the world and the way we are seeded in the depths of our selves.

Fate is purpose seen from the other end of life. When engaged with the true aim of one's life, looking back can be revelatory. In the end, very little is lost. Once the key is found and the door of the self opens, it all makes sense; the ascents and descents, even the tragedies and failures can be revalued. When the door between the worlds begins to swing, the values of time and place are altered and everything can have renewed meaning.

LADDERS OF THE HEART

An old Hasidic parable takes up the issues of ladders and the soul from a very different angle. That legend depicts a long ladder that originates in heaven and reaches all the way down to the surface of the earth. In order to be born and enter life here on earth, each soul must descend down the rungs of the heavenly ladder. When the time of birth arrives and the first arc of life begins, the ladder disappears altogether. Throughout the rest of our life on earth there is a subtle feeling that we are incomplete and that something is missing. Meanwhile, the legend says, up in heaven they are continually "calling home the souls" who have descended and therefore long to return to heaven again.

The story can help explain the sense of longing common to the human heart and the anguish we can feel at having lost the divine connection. The usual lesson drawn from the tale is that we are all lost souls until we find a way to ascend again and return to the heavenly realm. Yet, there is another way to view the ladder between heaven and earth and the longings in the human soul.

Another old tradition suggests that rather than ascending in order to find fulfillment, we are actually here to bring heaven down to earth. Our souls are always longing to find home; yet home is also where the heart is and the human heart may find a home in both realms. Some longing must have pulled the soul down to earth to begin with; being stretched between the divine and earthly things seems to be a big part of human nature.

Despite the promise of so many forms of proselytizing and advertising, the point of human existence cannot simply be the making of a steady ascent. In order for the soul to fully awaken, both ascent and descent are needed. Wholeness involves descent as well as ascent; the heights of spirit and the depths of soul; falling down as well as rising above the mess. Wisdom requires both as well, the call to spirit and the pull of soul. Without the shading of soul what could be wise becomes too sure of itself, too certain of the way, and too blinded by the light. Without the lift and light of spirit, soul can become too heavy, too tragic, or self-absorbed, or too stuck in the mud to move anything forward. Only when these two movements become combined can we gradually generate a deep enough sense of self that can unite the opposing energies of life.

Ascent can lift us up and "show us the way;" it can reveal the purpose of our lives and the destiny we are aimed at. Descent however, makes the inner connection real as it relates the pulse of the body with the longings of the soul. Spirit may long to ascend to the heavens above, but the soul wants a further incarnation, a deepening down and true grounding here on earth. Wisdom seeks a path that makes each person whole by following both the upward call of spirit and the downward pull of soul.

The two arcs can also be viewed as two necessary adventures in life; the first adventure aimed more at facing up to the life one has been given, and the second adventure shaping an inner life and learning of how to live from the vital gradient in one self. First, we must go forth and risk life in the body; be fully present and engaged in the life of the times. Secondly, we must fully face the results in our mind and in our soul and turn inward to find the thread of the second adventure within. It is not simply a matter of having experiences in life, but also of setting life experiences within the narratives of the soul; only then can experience give birth to genuine meaning.

As modern people, we tend to be too focused on ascension, and the need to succeed and rise above has become an obsession. We suffer a loss of soulfulness and earthliness and a disconnection from the imaginative roots of our souls. Spirit and soul are reflections of each other, each necessary for holding the life-tension that sustains the living world. There are times when the world goes out of balance, times when it is in the interest of human nature as well as great nature to bring the touch of the divine down to earth again. At such times, taking the risks of the second arc of revelation and realization becomes more important than ever.

THE SOUL'S ADVENTURE

The soul needs an outer drama that can help awaken the inner myth that it carries and the original agreement it made before descending to earth. Throughout the course of life, the soul will create impossible dramas and persistent dilemmas in order to crack open the shell of the little-self and reveal the living seed, the original agreement, it carries within. The soul's great adventure becomes the focus of the arc of return, which shifts our attention from the outer world to the deep self and soul within.

Meanwhile, so much of life is merely the life of a "personality" playing on the little stage of familiar things. Under the little-self's rule, we try to control our environment and settle in some pseudo-safety, which keeps us both small and unrevealed. The little-self seeks a harmless world that can be measured and kept under control. Yet, the deeper murmurs of the heart and soul ever long for something wildly other from our expected selves. What we really seek is the greater self and deeper soul originally set within us.

The second arc of life requires a renewed willingness to risk life all over again. This arc of return involves a descent as well as a turning back to the original source of life; it involves a deep sense of turning inward that alone can turn everything around. Whereas the ego must develop and grow along the first arc of life, on the second arc the ego must bow down and accept a diminished role relative to the forgotten-self, which waits below and within to be recognized.

Something original in the soul desires to risk body and mind by following the second arc, which can reveal hidden meanings and provide surprising healing. From the view of the soul, each crossroads or crisis in life offers opportunities, not simply to change, but to completely transform our lives. At every threshold there are unseen creative energies waiting to enter the world through the awakening of our souls.

Each meaningful step we take on the path of life involves some tension between the needs of the common world and the dreams of the soul. Often, the choice comes down to adventure or complacency. Since life is rarely neutral, complacency does not simply lead to stasis but to decay and increasing loss of life purpose. We must step outside our given personality and work beyond the expected idea of our self in order to uncover the unknown, yet original self.

We must risk our known self repeatedly so that, on the soul's surprising adventure, we find an unexpected self, a self that was unknown. This inner sense and deeper self is not "self-conscious," but rather more clearly conscious of who we are intended to be in both spirit and in soul.

Ultimately, the heart of the human drama concerns the question of whether we are moving toward a greater life or away from it. Either we are growing more soul and becoming a greater vessel for the flow of life, or we are shrinking from life and secretly feeding our blind instincts and the realm of hungry ghosts. The obstacles, dilemmas, and losses we encounter in life's unending drama either cause us to grow bigger, and thus lead greater lives, or else become smaller people.

On the arc of realization the style tends to be more revelation than indoctrination, more a process of uncovering what is already there than following general doctrines or systems of belief.

Amidst the flood of changes, mass confusions, and the great

forgetting already underway, the awakening of the innate character and purpose of the soul becomes increasingly important for both the individual and society. The lack of coherence and orientation in the outside world makes the inborn seeds of the soul and our inherent sense of purpose more critical than ever.

The original agreement of the soul forms the inner shape and precise aim of each life. It is the inner dream of our soul, the pattern that brought us to life in the first place, and the core imagination waiting to awaken and blossom from within. Without that soul agreement, we can be like anyone else; when in touch with it, we can't help but be who we were originally intended to be.

This original agreement cannot be dismissed or replaced, for it involves the divine source of our lives as well as the aim of our individual existence. Although it is forgotten at birth, remains mostly invisible in childhood, and may be denied throughout one's life, the first agreement cannot be erased from the soul. Despite having meaningful responsibilities to others, the original agreement of the soul remains the primary obligation and deepest responsibility of our lives.

The soul's great adventure involves finding and germinating the seeds within and undertaking the mission encoded in them. The first agreement is indelible; it is the source of our deepest capacity to change, but it does not change. Each time we remember a piece of why we came to life, we pull the seeds of eternity further into the world of time. Through the vehicle of consciousness we can become unique translators of the flow of divine knowledge.

In his continuing efforts to help people understand how change is the only thing that can be constant in this world, Heraclitus turned from fire to water. He pointed out how no one "ever steps in the same river twice;" for it cannot be the same river and we can never be the same person as before. He added that, "Even a soul submerged in sleep is hard at work and helps make something of the world." Imagine how much more we can help the world change and heal if we become more awake to the core meaning and true aim of our own souls.

Heraclitus also suggested that, "in changing we find purpose." The point is not starting from a blank slate, but renewing from the inner spark and living flame of life set within each of us. Physically and metaphysically we are made of the stuff of dreams, sparks of the original fire that that started the whole universe. We are born of the constant heat of creation and ongoing flux of life. Yet, without genuine imagination and a sense of the subtle presence of soul, we are unable to imagine ourselves as having meaning and contributing to the work of creation ongoing.

In the underlying unity of life, what is true for the soul is also true for the Soul of the World. The world, despite all its troubles, remains a place of ongoing creation. Creation wishes to continue, yet in certain ways the flame of creation can only work through the souls of those alive at a given time.

CHAPTER 9

TURNING THINGS AROUND

Our dominant ideas often become millstones rather than pole stars.

There's an old story that tells how an entire culture forgot the importance of having people grow old with dignity and become genuine elders. Not only did the people forget, but they also created a law that required older folks to abandon their lives once they reached a certain age. Although I found the story a long time ago, I have to confess that I became more interested in it when I began to feel the effects of aging myself. Yet as the story will illustrate, the issue of abandonment is not just a concern for older people. Rather, the greater issue involves how forgetting important things about life can lead to a growing sense of abandonment that can affect people of all ages.

What first drew me to the story was its unusual title: "The Sixty Canyon Abandonment." As it turns out, the number sixty in the title has nothing to do with the amount of canyons involved. Rather, it names the age at which a person was required to abandon their life and wander out into the distant canyons to die alone. This may seem an outlandish and far-fetched idea; yet people abandon themselves all the time. People at all stages of life can be seen to abandon their true longings and genuine dreams.

Some people have such a fear of life that they abandon all attempts at fully living. Others become lost in clouds of nostalgia, longing so much for times past that they abandon the present moment. Modern people abandon themselves to mass media, personal devices, and become lost in all kinds of entertainment. Everyone can be said to have abandonment issues and every culture at some point forgets what is most important. The old story of the canyons of abandonment serves as a reminder that the true aims and values of life can be easily forgotten, and people can feel abandoned at any age.

The story begins in a country ruled by a warlord whose main interests involved making people more productive and making preparations for war. Like many who see power as a way to dominate others, this autocratic ruler was also known for creating laws intended to satisfy an immediate need or even indulge his own whims. Since making war and producing goods were the primary activities of the realm, the ruler reasoned that by the age of sixty, people were less able to contribute to the collective effort. Soon enough, a law was passed that required everyone reaching sixty years of age to vacate their lives, give up all they had, and leave behind everyone they knew. Simply because of aging, older people had trek out to a distant mountain canyon and, once there, abandon themselves to death.

Despite the callous nature of the practice, once the idea of abandonment became the law of the land, people followed the rule and gave up their lives when the time came. Someone looking in from the outside might quickly see the brutality and absurdity of this local rule. However, once someone with power and authority lays down the law, most people will follow it. This should cause those who simply believe in the rule of law to consider more deeply.

Sometimes, the rule of law can serve to protect people; other times, laws can overrule people's better judgment and even their best interests. As an old proverb reminds, "Laws control a lesser person, while right conduct directs a greater people."

One day, it happened that a certain man had reached his sixtieth year. In order to be a law-abiding person, he would have to depart from life on the anniversary of his birth. In one sense, it was the day of his birth; in another, it was the beginning of the end for him. In his case, he had two grown children, a daughter and son who truly cared for him. When they saw their father preparing for the lonely walk into the distant canyons, they both became sad and troubled. When he expressed resignation, stating matter of factly that "the law is the law," they insisted that they would at least go with him on his last journey.

So they all set out together on the path of abandonment. They had gone some distance and reached a place where they had to climb a winding forest path when the children noticed something odd. Their father kept clipping off the tips of evergreen branches and tossing the tips onto the path behind them. The sister and brother stopped the old man to say that they could see what he was trying to do. They pointed out that it made no sense for him to mark the path so he might find his way back to the village. He would only be breaking the law and was sure to be publicly punished before being sent away again.

The father answered calmly, saying he understood that he was now old and near the end of the trail anyway. If he became lost, it would not be a great loss. However, they were young and had their whole lives ahead of them. It would be a disaster if they became disorientated and could not find their way back to life. He was marking the path so that they would not lose their way and wind up becoming abandoned themselves.

The children could feel their hearts breaking a little as they all stood together on the deserted trail. Sensing the compassion and gentleness in their father's heart, they realized that they could not abandon him in that way. In that moment, which may have felt like a lifetime, they all realized that they were in this trouble together. They were beginning to see how abandoning life at any stage could begin to drain life from all stages. Despite what the law required, the son and daughter now insisted that the old father return with them. Feeling relieved for the moment, they all turned around and the younger ones led the way back to the village.

Upon arriving at their simple hut, the children realized that their father would have to go into hiding. Seeing no other option, they loosened some floorboards and made a place for the father to hide in the earth below the house. No one knew that the old man had not abandoned life except for the young ones, and they had no intention of telling anyone. Not knowing what might come from breaking the law, they kept close to each other. Each day, the children would pass food to the father and comfort him. For his part, the old man had begun living not just under the house, but also outside the law.

THE TURNING POINT

There is more to come in the old tale, but it seems wise to stop —just as the old man and his children in the story—and consider the situation. In trying to understand what might turn things around in contemporary culture, I keep thinking of this point in the story. Modern society seems hell bent on rushing into disaster, both in terms of creating environmental troubles and in abandoning core values of human culture. The failure of institutions along with the lack of knowing elders and guides has made the world far more perilous. In terms of abandonment, it seems that we are in a life and death situation ourselves.

Human culture seems increasingly at odds with the rhythms of nature and modern mass societies keep forgetting what life is really about. In the contemporary situation, people of all ages can feel there is no purpose to life and anyone can feel lost and rejected at any time. We may be in a modern predicament, but at the same time be in a folk tale condition. Like characters in a fateful story we have to find ways to turn things around or else abandon ourselves to an increasingly diminished future.

In the story, a moment of mutual awakening occurs when the young and the old manage to stop in time and consider what is happening to them. At one level, the father seems ready to abandon life and simply let nature take its course. Yet, in facing his own death a realization dawns upon him and a depth of compassion awakens in him. He cannot simply abandon his children or neglect the future which, as young people, they represent. The motif of marking the way home appears in many folk and fairy tales. Most often, it is the young ones who try to mark the trail in order to find their own way home. Here, the old man acts as an elder who remembers how easily people become lost in this world and need guidance to find their way.

The old man may be willing to accept his own abandonment, but he cannot accept that his children might become disoriented and lose their way in life. This might be the first clue as to how things could begin to turn around. The next clue comes when the young ones have their own moment of compassion and greater understanding. In the midst of the path of abandonment, a deepening of understanding and an awakening of compassion develops amongst young and old alike. In awakening to a deeper truth in a heartfelt way, they begin to reverse the common attitudes that have come to be the law of the land.

In some sense, the march of time becomes reversed and even renewed, as a seeming dead end becomes a new beginning. The moment of realization turns the father from simply being an older person to being an elder. The transformation comes not from a social event or religious ceremony; rather, it comes from an inner awakening of the heart and soul. Once again, the solution to life's outer dilemmas comes from an inward experience of one's own soul. Even if ceremonies for converting older people to elders did exist, the actual change must occur inside the souls of those involved. If there is no change at the level of the soul, there will be no change at the level of collective culture.

A true turnaround in life moves us beyond our current understanding of both ourselves and the world we live in. As in the story, when a person truly "turns their life around" it also affects those who are around them. When the older one in the situation does not ignore or forget the young ones, they cannot manage to simply forget him either. His caring for them causes them to realize how they truly care for him. Soon, they all realize that they care more deeply for life and for each other than the rule of law or the current trends of society can understand. In this world, essential things about life keep being forgotten; yet no amount of rules or laws can replace the presence of genuine wisdom and compassion.

IMPOSSIBLE TASKS

When we return to the story, the young people have knowledge that they must keep to themselves, at least for the time being. At the same time, the old man must conceal himself while he considers everything happening in the world from a deeper place than others. As time went on, the daughter and son returned to their usual ways of life, while the old man adjusted to living under the house. Then, the ruler of the realm became more extreme in his demands. He started making new rules and odd ultimatums without consultation with anyone, and the common folks suffered increasing levels of confusion, anxiety, and hardship.

When it seemed that things could not get any worse, the lord of the land called a general assembly and declared that anyone who could not fulfill certain tasks would pay a harsh penalty. Everyone became troubled and even more confused when he announced that the first task required each of them to bring him a rope made of ashes. Anyone who could not or would not complete the task would receive a serious penalty.

Of course, no one had any idea of how to make a rope with ashes. The son and daughter came back to their hut anguishing over the impossible task and the penalties facing everyone. From under the house, the old man could hear them talking and asked what was causing all the concern. Upon learning the nature of the task, he told the son and daughter to find a length of tightly woven rope. He advised them on how to slowly burn the rope so that it kept its shape while being turned to ash. He showed them how to protect the ash rope from the wind while bringing it to the ruler.

The lord of the land was surprised. He did not expect that anyone would be able to solve the puzzle. His intent was simply to create a sense of chaos and dominate the people while becoming richer at the expense of everyone else. Although he had to acknowledge the daughter and son of the old man for being clever, the ruler immediately set another troublesome task upon all the people. The new executive order required each person to bring a conch shell through which a silken thread had been thoroughly passed. Again, whoever failed to accomplish the task would have to pay a harsh penalty.

This time, the daughter and son brought the dilemma directly to their father under the house. Once again, the elder told them not to worry and to find a conch shell, an ant, a silken thread, and a grain of rice. The old man had them tie the rice to the end of the thread and place it well inside the shell. Then, placing the ant inside the shell, he aimed the opposite end at the sun. The children were amazed at how quickly the ant appeared at the other end of the nautilus carrying the grain of rice, but also pulling the thread all the way through the twists of the shell.

The next day, the children were the only ones who had solved the riddle and accomplished the task. The lord was impressed but lost no time in assigning a third task: everyone must bring him a drum that played itself or else be fined for failing the test. Of course, the son and daughter quickly brought the seemingly impossible task to the attention of the old man. He asked them to catch a bumble bee and bring him a clay pot as well. After emptying the pot, the old man placed the bee inside and closed the top by stretching a piece of leather over it.

When the children handed the pot to the ruler, the bee began to buzz around and bump against the top. The effect was that the pot seemed to be a drum somehow playing itself. At that point, the ruler insisted on knowing how the children could solve the puzzling tasks and do it so quickly. Not knowing what else to do, the children bowed before the lord and explained that it was their old father who had the knowledge of how to accomplish the seemingly impossible tasks. The ruler asked the age of the old man and why he did not present the solutions himself. The son and daughter had to admit that the old man was past the age of abandonment, and that they had broken the law.

When the ruler questioned why the old man remained in the village, the children explained how they could not abandon someone who was so caring, compassionate, and wise. The ruler quickly concluded that since they had broken the law, the solutions to the tasks were invalid and everyone needed to be punished. Then, to everyone's surprise, the ruler seemed to turn inward and ponder the unusual situation. After some time, he said he was impressed with the honesty and compassion of the children and surprised at the wisdom of the old man. He admitted that the rule requiring that old people be abandoned was in fact foolish, especially when, as elders, they might offer wisdom and guidance for the benefit of everyone. He exonerated the old man and asked that he come to court as an adviser.

From that moment, the Sixty Canyon Abandonment Law was itself abandoned and soon abolished. In its place, people began to consider ways to develop greater respect for those who were older; but also ways to involve younger people with their elders. Those who aspired to be elders began to work at what they determined was the second risk of life — being willing to risk what was left of their lives for the benefit of those who were younger and, thus, a better future for everyone. This second risk was deemed to involve sustaining the life of both nature and culture, while finding ways to keep everyone connected to the community of souls.

THE ARC OF RETURN

The old story has the would-be elder go over the hill on the path of abandonment, but then come back. Instead of fading away, he plays a key role in changing the life of the community. Part of what turns everything around is that the old man turns out to be more lively and attuned to life than he is expected to be. In order to not abandon what he considers most important in life, he must go against the mainstream and even learn to live outside the law. On the way back from the land of abandonment, the old man becomes not only an elder, but also a kind of "outlaw."

A genuine elder stands at least partially outside the social order and beyond the lines of civil authority. In that sense, there is a revelation that genuine elders are not simply the keepers of "law and order." Rather, the role of elders involves turning to higher laws and deeper truths in order to better see where the common laws and customs have abandoned those who the laws are intended to protect.

The idea of a genuine elder appears as the opposite of and the antidote to those who have power but use it unjustly. The ruler in the situation has "positional authority;" whereas the genuine elder has inner authority. One draws power from the established order and uses it for personal gain; the other draws upon a deeper sense of authenticity and uses that power for the benefit of others. One serves the demands of the moment and the needs of the little-self; the other serves an unseen future and the aims of the awakened soul. Elders turn their attention to true sources of power instead of clinging to power in the daily world.

The warlord in the story acts the familiar role of an autocrat and would-be strongman. He also represents what happens when a person uninitiated into the deeper sense of life has a position of authority. He has power, but no real idea what it might be intended to serve. He has authority, but only because he has a position to which people must submit. In a sense, the ruler plays the role of a "negative elder." He has the trappings of leadership without the vision or wisdom necessary for it to become meaningful. He has the means of power without the understanding and compassion necessary to make the means serve a genuine end. In the end, power that does not enhance life must eventually serve to destroy it.

On one level, people need the "rule of law" in order to have a sense of order and feel protected. On a deeper level, however, someone needs to be above the law when the common laws fail to protect the sanctity of life and neglect to serve those in genuine need. In traditional cultures, the elders are expected to remember the essential values and enduring truths that everyone else keeps forgetting. Elders serve a higher purpose as well as a deeper order of life. Genuine elders learn to see beyond the usual restrictions in order to uphold higher standards than those that happen to rule the day because of history, politics, or even uninspired religion.

The ancient tale of the canyons of abandonment is not simply about respecting older people, but also about the necessity of making elders. When a culture forgets its elders, the elders begin to forget themselves. Instead of becoming elders, people simply become "olders" who, as they age, forget what is most important in life. Wisdom cannot simply come from having life experience, and living longer does not mean becoming wiser. In fact, the opposite can be true, as some people never grow up and others become more fearful and foolish as they age. Instead of having answers to the essential questions of life, older people can become a growing question mark themselves.

Elders are examples of those who die before they die. They face death consciously and develop a greater appreciation for life. It's not simply that they desire to live longer, but they also have a longing to serve and enhance all of life. As a representative of things outside the norms and beyond social limits, an elder becomes more of a guide than a leader, more of a deep resource than a frontrunner.

Growing older happens to everyone, but growing wiser happens to those who awaken to a greater sense of meaning and purpose in life. Elders can carry a greater vision of life because they have developed insight into their own lives. They faced up to whatever fate had in store for them and found ways not simply to survive, but also to understand the intricacies and struggles of human life. Turning things around on a cultural level requires individuals to turn within to face the soul and find forgotten things worth risking the rest of their lives for. In many traditions, the elders speak for the animals and the forests as well as the ancestors. Thus, the return of elders can also mean a return of the living world of nature as well as a return of the sacred sense of life.

The return of the elder illustrates two important ideas about the course of human life. First of all, the presence of a genuine elder demonstrates that "old age" is not simply an afterthought or an appendage to a life already lived. The process of aging can involve both meaning and purpose if a person is growing wiser while growing older. An old African proverb states that, "White hair does not make the elder." Everyone grows older, but not everyone becomes the wiser for it.

Secondly, the idea that an elder serves something not simply traditional, but truly transcendent shows that life can have significance beyond the typical scope of the individual. The elders act from a conscious sense that they will die, but also the knowledge that life will continue. Those who continue to grow as they grow older are able to develop long-term vision where most become blinded by issues and common needs that are closer at hand. Those who truly become "old enough to know better" also become living depositories of wisdom for the next generation to draw upon. In that sense, they develop "inner authority" that knows what needs to be preserved and remembered in order for human life to be noble, meaningful, and in tune with nature.

Elders lead by remembering further back than others as well as by seeing more clearly ahead. Therefore, they are less likely to try to be political leaders and more likely to become cultural and spiritual guides. The elders serve as "seers" who can see behind and beyond the politics of the day and perceive the important needs of the future. Elders hold to the universal laws and the highest ideals of humanity; in that sense, genuine elders are also instinctive humanitarians. In traditional cultures, the elders were considered to be a valuable resource without whose guidance the whole society could lose its way.

AGING VS GROWING DOWN

Old age alone cannot make the elder, for the qualities most needed involve more than the natural process of physical change. Rather than abandon themselves to the effects of old age, elders choose instead to grow wiser as they inevitably grow older. To truly grow older means to grow deeper and wiser; not simply to step down or step aside for others, but to descend to deeper places of understanding.

Becoming wiser requires using insight to deepen experience, a kind of "growing down" from the surface issues of life to places of deeper understanding. Amidst the inevitable troubles of life, the bubble of the "closed ego" bursts and a deeper, wiser self is born. Such psychological maturity involves a shift from a self-centered life to one of genuine meaning and greater service to others.

In modern life, instead of people growing "older and wiser," people can simply grow older and older. Instead of developing wise and seasoned elders who can help others find meaningful ways to live, modern societies tend to produce unenlightened "olders" who blindly seek ways to hold onto life at any cost. However, no amount of social security will convert the olders into elders, just the way that no amount of information can change knowledge into wisdom. If maturity generates greater vision, it leads to wisdom; if not, maturity becomes degeneration.

Whoever said that age brings wisdom had probably not lived long enough to see how often it can bring fear and narrow-mindedness. People more often repeat the past and fear the future rather than develop the greater vision and deeper understanding of life that constitutes wisdom. When older folks fail to recommit to the great ideals that sustain the deepest values of human life, they tend to feel more fearful and anxious while also becoming more cynical and self-involved. It is one thing to lament the lack of "adults in the room," and quite another to realize the lack of genuine elders needed to envision a meaningful way of life. People are fond of saying that youth may be "wasted on the young;" but in today's world, living longer can be wasted on those who simply grow older without being any wiser for it.

In the story "The Sixty Canyon Abandonment," the old man winds up living down in the darkness, under the house and under the village as well. This implies dwelling deeper within, but also means to willingly enter the unconscious. His underground dwelling symbolizes getting below the confusions of the daily world in order to have a deeper perspective on the conflicts and dilemmas affecting everyone at the level of community. Descent was the way of the soul at the beginning, in the end it is the way to genuine wisdom. The old man becomes the elder under the house; he also becomes the village elder who can better understand the underlying problems of the community.

The first requirement of life involves growing up; but becoming a real "grown-up" requires growing down, descending into the depths of the soul and deepening the understanding of life and one's genuine place in it. The term "growing old" indicates that there can be another way of growing besides "growing up." The elder in a person is found by "growing down," by becoming deeper and therefore closer to understanding life. Of course, *understanding* suggests getting down below as well — standing under the surface of common reality in order to see things from a deeper, wiser perspective. Wisdom is more about roots than branches, more about finding deeper ways to be and to see. Elders, then, become "more fully descended" — both more grounded in life and more anchored in the soul.

THE SECOND RISK OF LIFE

In the story of the Sixty Canyon Abandonment, the coalition of the elder and the young folks faces a series of seemingly impossible tasks that endanger the entire community. A rope that would normally be used to tie things with knots must be reduced to ashes and become vulnerable to the slightest wind. A thread must be pulled through the unseen intricacies of a nautilus shell, and a drum must appear to play itself. When dealing with problems that seem impossible, some things must be looked at the opposite way around, while other things must be seen from the inside out. Being willing to descend into the depths of the psyche becomes necessary if the riddles of life are to be solved.

When faced with an impossible task, a wise person allows the force of universal imagination to operate through them. Genuine imagination must come into play and help must come from unlikely places. In the story, tiny beings like ants and bees had to be sought as helpers, as if to indicate that a different order of understanding must be applied. The great problems in life involve conflicts and oppositions that cannot be solved at the surface of life. Yet, a hidden unity underlies all of life. In the depths of the soul things that otherwise are distinct opposites can also become the key to hidden unities.

Traditional tales from many cultures try to show how youth and elders are opposite sides of a psychic pairing that can help reveal an important secret of our human identity. They are parts of a paradox in which each is necessary to understand the other, and each holds a key to a deeper appreciation of the course of human life. Despite the common gaps between youth and elders, they are secretly connected, and each holds an essential piece of the human inheritance. The eternal youth carries the original dream of our life and our intrinsic vitality needed for living fully. The elder, or the inner sage, is intended to serve as a knowing guide through the troubles of the world. Like the wise old man or wise old woman in folk and fairytales, the inner guide can connect us to the deep human instincts for survival, but also help us discover new ways to find paths of meaning and purpose.

At the point in the story when the old man and the young sister and brother refuse to abandon each other, they also take a big risk together. They enter a secret alliance that involves the second risk of life. First, we must risk having a life — finding a way into life and facing up to obstacles we encounter in the world. The second risk in life involves becoming present in one's inner life and awakening to the nature of one's being. The second risk involves making a genuine interior life, something that modern education and mass culture do not prepare us to do.

Because the second level of risk is avoided and misunderstood, risk becomes primarily associated with youthful exploits and heroic adventures. Risking one's life comes to mean being exposed to external dangers rather than being willing to risk following the calling of one's soul. As in the abandonment story, the second risk of life involves risking oneself for the sake of sustaining life in ways that go beyond oneself. When older folks risk living with genuine courage and vision, young people feel encouraged to find and follow their own ideals and live their dreams. Without this risk, we grow older than we need to be and become hollow inside by virtue of having abandoned our genuine ideals.

In many traditions, elders and youth were considered to have a foot in each world in a way that gives them authenticity and "edge of life" relevance. Each inhabits a betwixt and between state that can make them radically open to the spirit of change. As a result, they can be more in touch with the otherworld, but not out of touch with the struggles in this world. The dynamic of awakening the underlying soul can be seen in the shape of a secret alliance of the young and the old. Together they shape the inner imagination needed to face the impossible tasks and survive troubled times. When the oldest and the youngest in the soul come together, we can awaken the living force of the underlying unity of life.

The arc of imagination that secretly generates and sustains human culture stretches between the eternal youth and the wise sage, the inner guide or the "old soul" that secretly resides in the heart of each person. The dream of life on earth depends upon a conscious connection between these ancient and endlessly creative qualities of the human soul. It is not that childhood doesn't matter or that the period of adulthood is somehow dismissible. Rather, it is that the child is unwittingly carrying an inner dream that will try to awaken during the struggles of youth, and the adult feeling the burdens of responsibility is close to waking the sage in their heart.

Youth and elders do not simply represent the extremes of life; when functioning as "awakened outsiders," they become the channels through which new ideas as well as old forms of wisdom try to enter the common world. If we but turn around amidst the rush of life, we can find that two things are trying to catch up to us at the same time: the knowing inner sage and the ever-young, dream-making youth of the soul. Each offers an essential part of the great adventure of life, which is intended to be lived fully, creatively, and passionately all the way to the end. Together they can create an awakening of the collective soul that can turn things around even after a period of great loss and collective abandonment.

CHAPTER 10

THE BIRD OF TRUTH

Threads of meaning and truth are present in everyone, but may only become visible when something creative is attempted.

What people now call the "real world," or the realm of time and space, used to be known as the "front of the world." What generates all that we consider reality used be known as the "world behind the world," the timeless realm that originally produced and continues to sustain the time-bound world. Everything that comes to be in this world comes from the unseen center and hidden wellspring of living forms, which was also known as the *Anima Mundi*, or the Soul of the World.

Everything connected to the world behind this world is meaningful, both full of meaning and also eternal. When we are inspired, it is the breath of the otherworld that has lifted our spirit and opened the inner eyes of our soul. While in touch with this otherness — that is also a part of us — life becomes vibrant, vital, and imbued with meaning. When out of touch with the unseen realm that is both beyond and within us, everything can seem empty, pointless, and altogether meaningless.

We live in a time of worldwide upheaval and impending dangers—radical climate change, a deepening humanitarian crisis of rampant injustice, and a loss of compassion and understanding.

At the same time, there is a crisis of meaning and truth that imperils the heart and soul of human culture. Humanity is suffering a growing dissociation from its own inner nature. The deep disconnect from soul can be termed the collective wound of humanity at this time. Because humans are secretly tied to the Soul of the World, the loss of soul not only diminishes the sense and meaning of human life, it also essentially damages the world.

The great ache in the modern world, like the deeper sufferings within each soul, cannot be cured by a new drug or another technological invention. Imagination is the missing ingredient most needed to turn things around and truly change the dire conditions that prevail on earth at this time. Without genuine imagination and a sense of the subtle presence of soul, we are unable to imagine ourselves surviving the troubles we face and contributing to the work of creation ongoing.

Imagination is the living bridge that connects the two realms; anything that comes to life in this world must first be imagined. As the deepest power of the human soul, imagination also connects each person born on earth to the Soul of the World. When the troubles in this world become overwhelming, the solutions can only be found in the endless resources of the unseen realm that turns out to be behind everything, and within us as well. When great troubles abound, whether it be on the world stage or at a critical stage of a person's life, what we need is the touch of imagination and a hint of the eternal. It is when the power of imagination becomes diminished that people cannot envision ways through the conflicts and dilemmas of life.

Meaning is an expectation of the human soul, and the real work of the soul is to help awaken life to its meaning. Each person is a mystery until they become revealed. And the mystery at the center of each soul is secretly tied to the mysterious center of the cosmos. Each time an individual soul awakens to a genuine sense of meaning and purpose, there is more presence in the world and more meaning and truth in life.

There is an old story told by elders amongst the Bushmen in Central Africa that shows how a moment of awakening can alter the course of a person's life and also shift the meaning of the world. A long time ago, in a valley near an ancient lake, there lived a hunter who went out each day seeking wild birds in the woods and fowl in the marshes. He was well known for his hunting skills and capacity to provide people of his village with food. While out hunting one day, he bent down to drink from a wide pool in the heat of the afternoon. As he gazed into the water, he suddenly saw the reflection of a great white bird in the sky above him. He looked up quickly, but the bird was already out of sight.

In the wonder of that moment, a burning desire came over him to see the magnificent bird again. He waited near the pool all day, constantly watching the skies. Only when nightfall came and chased the light away did he return home. He arrived in his village carrying an empty bag and appearing to be in a dark mood. The next day, he did not set out to hunt as he always did, but sat in silence as if he had become a brooding bird himself. When people asked what caused this change in his mood and demeanor, he said nothing, and simply sat in silence.

When his friend asked what ailed him, he described the vast white bird with outstretched wings that shined in the endless blue sky. His friend said it must have been a beam of sunlight playing on the surface of the water that was now playing tricks with his mind. The hunter simply answered that he wanted nothing else but to have another vision of that transcendent bird. Soon after that, he gave up hunting for game entirely. Some people said that he had lost his way; others claimed that he wished to do what others could not and make himself out to be a seer or a wonder. Eventually, people simply left him alone to brood, and he did not protest.

One day, he left behind all that he had and everyone that he knew and set out into the wide world in search of the bird that had come to him as a beatific vision. He sought after it in the forests and in the woods, by the lakes and in the rushes, but never caught sight of the bird he had glimpsed for only the briefest moment in time. Everywhere he went, he asked if anyone had seen the bird or knew of it. Although some did say they knew of it, no one had seen the bird in a long while.

After a long time, during which he had grown old with searching, he came to a place at the edge of a wide valley. When he asked about the shining bird, the people there said that it was known to nest at the top of the great mountain that stood across the plain. He asked what the name of the bird might be, and they said people called it the Bird of Truth.

The hunter lost no time in crossing the plain and beginning to climb the mountain. However, the sides of it were steep and he soon found himself to be exhausted. As he lay on a ledge unable to move, he looked up at the blue sky and suddenly felt a great despair. It was the same endless sky in which the great creature had first appeared, but no bird was to be seen. As he lay still and felt there was no use in further striving, he realized he was about to die. Looking up one more time, he saw a lone white feather floating down toward where he lay. He stretched out his hand and grasped it and holding that single feather, he died content.

Sometimes you can quickly tell that a story is truly old because it strikes somewhere deep in the soul, the way the feather falling at just the right moment redeems an entire life. A feather is a light thing; its hollow core is filled with air and it is easily lifted by the wind. Yet, a feather can represent the entire truth of a person's life and reveal how the human soul remains secretly connected to the Soul of the World. Whether it appears as a symbol of truth or beauty, the feather of imagination is so light as to be imperceptible, so fleeting as to be easily forgotten; yet so important as to transcend all other needs.

The story begins with a hunter whose skills are recognized and valued by everyone because he can face great difficulties and provide sustenance at the basic levels of life. He represents the archetypal hunter in the human psyche with all the ancient instincts for tracking and hunting, for honing survival skills and providing food and shelter. However, the ancient soul of humanity harbors a greater sense of longing and a deeper sense of hunger that can be just as essential to our survival as food. Something deep within us needs a different order of nourishment — a food not for the body, but for the soul.

Like the pairing of the youth and elder, the hunter represents another paradox found in the depths of the human soul. What on one hand can be a tough-minded hunter dead set on finding game; can on the other hand be found to be a tender-minded seeker on the trail of truth and beauty. Throughout the ages, humans have proven to be both tough-minded and tender-minded. To this day, tough-minded attitudes engender instincts for survival as well as tendencies toward rational approaches and practical solutions. By contrast, the tender-minded attitude tends to be more imaginative and intuitive, more tuned to feeling than thought. Being both mythical and poetic, the tender-minded perspective is connected to timeless things and transcendent visions.

The story of the Bird of Truth is an ancient one, passed down among people who were known to be great hunters and crafty survivors able to withstand the most difficult life circumstances. They knew better than most that there are hard times when we must draw upon the instinctive capacity to simply survive and tough things out. However, they also knew that there are dark times, in both individual and collective life, when the other hunter — the true seeker in the heart of humanity — must awaken to the calling of truth and beauty, or else everyone might lose their way and wind up empty-handed as well as hollow inside. On a psychological level, we each inherit a mixture of the two attitudes, as both tough and tender ways of being are necessary for survival and for finding ways to sustain and revitalize human culture.

The quest for truth and meaning is as ancient and natural as the hunt for food and shelter. Truth and beauty are places of refuge for the heart and soul of humanity, no matter what the circumstances of outer life might be. An ancient idea states that each person is guaranteed at least one moment of awakening to the core imagination set within the soul. This moment, in which the soul awakens and opens to the presence of beauty and truth, can come at any time. In the tale of the hunter, the awakening of the underlying soul comes as he bends over a pool in bright daylight.

All he sees in the life-changing moment of reflection is a fleeting image appearing in the sky and in the water at the same time. The vision of the shining bird is an epiphany that opens him to the eternal world behind the evident world. The thrill of the hunt silently shifts to a quest for something more elusive, yet ultimately more satisfying, to the soul. In a moment of deep awakening, the ancient hunter of game becomes the timeless seeker after truth, beauty, and spiritual fulfillment.

LIVING IN TRUTH

The story of the hunter offers a timeless and stunning example of a moment in which a person undergoes a complete metamorphosis. It also delivers a message about the capacity of the human soul to awaken to a deeper sense of life at any moment. The old Greek word for just such a sudden and complete change of awareness and intention is metanoia. More than a simple switch of attitude or a shift of interest, an experience of metanoia calls for an about-face, a complete change in the direction of life. *Meta* means "beyond," as in *metamorphosis* or *metaphysical*, while *noia* carries the sense of a "true understanding." A genuine turn-around in life moves us beyond our current understanding of both ourselves and the world in which we live.

The human soul is capable of such a radical sense of change that we can suddenly reach a place of understanding that had previously been beyond our comprehension. Such a thorough awakening involves not just a change of mind, but also a change of heart, which leads to a greater understanding of one's essence and reason for being. A thorough change of mind, one that also moves the heart, is often needed at critical moments in life. This kind of awakening moves the mind closer to the heart; especially closer to the thought and image that waits within our heart to be discovered. For, there is a thought in the heart, just as there are feelings in the mind. To truly know something by heart includes feeling it as well as thinking it.

This ancient sense of transformation assumes that there is something essential within us that we can turn to and learn from; that we can draw upon repeatedly and grow from continuously. Besides involving a change in consciousness, such a deep inner change also includes a process of self-healing that can occur in moments of wholeness arising from the source of the deep self and soul within us. The old reason for not giving up on someone, even if they have failed repeatedly, is because a genuine turnaround in life is possible at any time and at any age. Because such moments are timeless, when it comes to waking up and turning things around, it is never too late.

Being open enough to recognize an authentic moment of awakening is the first part of the challenge. After that, there is the struggle to stay awake and not forget what stirred us to the depths of our being. The hunter goes through a period of being lonely and feeling forlorn before he can fully accept that he must surrender to the transformation that has begun in his soul. Mythical stories are timeless, so that the time it takes to accept the full impact of a radical change of heart and soul can be any length of time. The event that changes a life forever can happen in a moment, but the point at which we truly surrender to it can be a long time coming. Like the ancient hunter, we can have a hint of what our soul truly longs for or a glimpse of the path our heart would have us follow, and yet feel unable to surrender to it. We can find ourselves feeling moody and out of touch for long periods of time until we accept that our entire life must change in order to follow what our heart knows to be true.

A meaningful change requires a genuine surrender to something that is mostly unknown. We must let go of what we thought our life was about in order to allow a new vision and a greater presence of spirit and soul to live within us. We must find ways to surrender to something greater than our usual sense of self, no matter how unsettling that can feel, no matter what others might think of us or expect from us. One way to understand the change of heart the hunter undergoes is that he now must find a way to be "living in truth."

In the old tale, the hunter's close friend tries to persuade him that what he saw with his own eyes was nothing but an illusion. All he saw was a flicker of light on the water; the rest is just his mind playing tricks on him. This somewhat cynical perspective depicts something that has become commonplace in the global village of the contemporary world, where people use "shiny objects" to distract everyone from the truth of the situation we are in. Whether it is the shiny new technological device being advertised or a political diversion being used to change the conversation, there are seemingly endless distractions that lead away from the genuine paths of truth and beauty. The increasing disorientation in modern culture makes it more difficult for everyone to find a genuine orientation to a life of meaning and purpose.

The struggle to awaken from the sleep of the daily world was there in ancient times, just as it can so commonly be found today. The greatest challenge has always been the risk of becoming ourselves in a world that is trying to turn us into everyone else. The problem now is that mass cultures diminish the very idea of the uniqueness of the individual soul. Even if we somehow manage to catch a glimpse of the kind of truth and beauty trying to enter the world through us, we can wind up feeling more alone, not less so. Only those friends who have managed to open to the spirit of their own lives can be able to relate to the ways in which we might struggle at the edge of genuine surrender. Even then, what we see and long for must be unique to us alone, and therefore can be confusing for others.

The story depicts how the hunter, after finally surrendering to the search for truth, sets out alone on the long path of discovery. The point is not that there can be no friends, teachers, or guides to meet along the way; hopefully there are many. The greater point is that even if there are helpful teachers and understanding friends, no one can travel a path of truth and beauty for us. No one else has seen the bird of truth in the same way—from the same angle, with the same eyes—as our own soul. Beauty and truth may be part of the natural heritage of the human soul, yet the way we each awaken to these inner treasures depends upon the uniqueness of our individual nature.

Despite the growing confusions and distractions of the modern world, we are the current inheritors of the deep human longings for truth and beauty and the life-sustaining capacity to transform. Each time we allow ourselves to be touched by the beauty of the world, to be stirred by the fleeting spirit of life, or be moved by something or someone that we love, we become the spiritual hunter at the edge of awakening. The question is always whether we will recognize what appears before us, beckoning us to change our lives. If we allow ourselves to be captured by the living imagination and surrender to it, we take another step on the path of the soul. Each time we take another step in the search for meaning and purpose, we are living in truth.

The ancient tale begins with an epiphany and ends with redemption. Like many old stories, it leaves out the specifics of what the seeker experiences and feels on the long path of becoming true to his soul. That gap is there for each of us to fill in with our own experiences of longing and loneliness, of seeking and trying to be true to ourselves. It can take a lifetime, or at least seem to take that long, before we can touch what was once only envisioned. Thus, the idea of living in truth can be hard to commit to and difficult to sustain, especially at this time, when the very ideas of truth and meaning are being questioned daily.

Some great confusion has fallen like a shadow across the world, a mass forgetting in which the sense of meaning waiting to be discovered right under the surface of life might be forsaken in favor of false claims and "big lies." People talk about a "post truth" world as if the repetition of big lies can erase the longing for truth and meaning that has been an essential part of humanity from the beginning. It is difficult to argue that we know the truth when we see it when so many people fall under the spells of cynicism and nihilism. A cynic is someone who once imagined ideals like truth and justice, but after some disappointment gave up on themselves. A nihilist is someone who, having failed to find anything redeeming in themselves, wishes to eradicate even the idea that meaning and truth can exist.

The core ideals of humanity are intended to serve as a light to follow, especially when the dark times come round and we become more exposed to the extremes of life and the winds of despair. The struggle for meaning and truth is also a battle for the presence and importance of the soul. Making more soul in the world leads to finding more meaning and more "lived truth."

The ancient Greek notion that *truth* means "not to forget" indicates how easy it can be to simply forget what is important in life. When the ideals of humanity are in danger, it is important to remember the old idea that, "Nothing but truth can hold the truth." In other words, we can only hold to ideals like truth, beauty and justice if we find ways to embody the truth of our own lives. Finding antidotes to the epidemic of lies, misinformation, and falsity means being willing to be open to radical changes while finding practices for living in truth.

LAW OF THE SOUL

Another ancient idea that supports the sense of living in truth can be found in the concept of "dharma," which permeates all the spiritual traditions of India. Although there is no simple translation in Western languages, the root meanings of dharma include the sense of holding and sustaining, and lead to ideas of justice and law — not outer law or man-made laws, but the cosmic laws and natural order that make the universe possible, and the inner law of the soul that makes human life meaningful.

Before birth, each individual receives a goal or destiny and a way of being to follow. Because each soul must be unique in some way, each person has a "sva-dharma" or "own law," the natural law and the true virtue of each life. Not virtue as a matter of doctrine or formal morality, but truth and justice as a lived experienced of one's inner nature and true way of being. This "law of one's being" also includes a sense of how each person might best serve the community of souls as well as the world. When in touch with the soul's inner nature and "own law," we can find the arts and practices, the aims and meanings that allow our souls to grow deeper, our imagination to expand, and our spirits to awaken more fully. Thus, to conform to what we already are at our life's core becomes the practice of dharma, or genuine service.

The ideas and practices of an inner dharma become important when the world goes out of balance and life becomes chaotic instead of orderly. Moral systems can be helpful in shaping collective customs and maintaining social order. However, when disorder prevails and truth and justice are threatened, no system of morality can serve as the key to sustaining the ideals of life. The transforming and healing power of truthfulness must be found in the form of "lived truth," which comes from the struggle to align oneself with the natural law and inner gradient of the individual soul. This is similar to the old admonition in the Western world: "To thine own self be true."

Finding and living out the pattern set within us means to follow the natural law of the soul that connects us to the cosmic order of life. Since each soul is part of the living organism of the universe, each person can become a conduit for universal energy. No one person or specific group has to take on the entire burden of the troubles of the world. In following our "own law" and learning to serve the natural dharma of the soul, we each become able to contribute to meaningful changes in the conditions of the world. It is in this way that living in truth becomes a practice that can change conditions when the world has gone wrong.

UNBURDENING THE HEART

Turning back to the tale of the Bird of Truth, the reason the hunter could die in a state of genuine contentment was that he had been living the truth of his own life, in his own way. There is an old idea that a person's life only makes sense when it is all over. Thus, the interpretation is not that the poor seeker only received a single feather of truth, which he only managed to find at the last minute. Rather, the fulfillment that the hunter felt at the end was the result of holding to the truth of his soul as best he could throughout his life. The single feather is the symbol of his "own law" and his unique connection to the eternal Bird of Truth.

He unburdened his heart by living out the life he had been given. He became as light as a feather because he responded to the calling of his soul and followed it all the way to the end. With his last gesture, he held onto the symbol of lived truth while releasing his hold on life. The synchronous moment in which the seeker releases his last breath while holding the feather of truth shows the potential unity between the individual soul and the natural order and living pulse of the cosmos.

This ancient and compelling image of holding the feather of truth remains part of the genuine heritage of the human soul. It is a reminder of the importance of living in truth. We must trust that there is meaning and purpose woven into our souls from the beginning, and that we may only learn the meaning of our own lives by living fully all the way to the end.

In the mysterious way of myth, the profound image of the hunter holding the feather from the Bird of Truth leads us all the way back to the myths of Egypt and the plight of the World Weary Man at the beginning of this book. Being weary from the harrowing conditions of the world and feeling despair at the loss of meaning in life, the ancient scribe considered giving up on life altogether. In that moment of deep uncertainty, his Ba-soul tries to convince him to return to his origins and pick up the inner thread, or original aim, of his life. His soul argues that if he lives life all the way to the end, they will cross the threshold between worlds together and he will find a true dwelling place in the afterlife.

One of the greatest scenes in all of mythology appears in depictions of the deceased person arriving in the otherworld and entering the hall of Maat, the Goddess of Truth. In ancient Egypt, Maat personified the concepts of truth, justice, and order in the world. The quintessential symbol of Maat was a single ostrich feather, known as the Feather of Truth.

Right after a person died, their heart would be placed on one side of a scale to be weighed against the single feather of Maat. If a person had lived a life that was in tune with their own soul, their heart would be unburdened and thus would be light enough to be in balance with the Feather of Truth. If that were the case, the person had realized the nobility of their soul and could pass onto the afterlife.

On the other hand, if the heart of the deceased was heavily burdened because they had not lived out the life their soul intended, had done serious harm, or simply died with too many unfinished issues, their soul's burdens would outweigh the Feather of Truth. In that case, a strange creature named the Devourer would consume the burdened heart and the deceased would have to go back and begin life over again.

In Egyptian myth, the heart was the key to both life on earth and the afterlife. The heart was identified as the seat of intelligence and understanding, the source of imagination, as well as the place of vital emotions. At the end of life, it would be the heart that needed to be examined and the heart would tell the whole story. Those who followed the inner law of their own soul and found ways to balance the energies of their heart were said to "live in Maat," which essentially means to be living in truth.

A psychological way of looking at the symbolism of an end-of-life judgment would be to consider it as an encounter with the deep self and soul that tries to become known to us throughout our life. Seen in this way, any moment in life can be the moment when we face our own soul and weigh ourselves against the truth that is trying to live into the world through us. An old idea considered that any time a person was connected to the meaning in their heart, they were "in balance" because they were in touch with their true nature. As an old saying asks, "Why wait until the end to learn what can become known right now?" Putting off the evaluation of the heart and soul only makes things weightier in the end.

The chamber where the final judgment takes place was called

the Hall of Two Truths because there was a statue of the Goddess of Truth at either end. There are many interpretations of what the two truths might be, and questions about why there are two truths instead of just one big truth. Having come toward the end of this book, I am weighing the two truths as dual aspects of redemption that can result from trying to live in the truth of our lives.

On one hand, if we are able to awaken to the inner truth of our souls and live out the meaning and aim that was in us from the beginning, we unburden our hearts. To the degree that we accomplish that, we become inheritors of the Feather of Truth. We become more balanced and can honestly meet the Goddess of Truth, or face our own self at the end of life. We can die, not just with dignity, but also with a touch of grace and nobility. We can let go at the end because we learned something about letting go and trusting something greater than the little-self along the way.

On the other hand, in so far as we manage to live in truth, we also find our "own dharma" and realize what we are intended to serve in this world. In contributing something meaningful to the world, we unburden our hearts in another direction. When a person, regardless of age, education or background, acts from the depths of their soul, they add imagination and meaning, unique presence, and beauty to the world. When we serve the aims of our souls, we make more soul in the world. And, in making more soul in this world, we strengthen the connection to the Soul of the World and help sustain the bridge between the worlds.

GOLDEN REPAIR OF THE WORLD

In the midst of all that threatens the earth and troubles our souls, what is trying to happen is metanoia on a global scale, a turnaround that awakens the soul in order to transform our hearts as well as our minds. The modern world has become fascinated with the workings of the brain, which is in fact an amazing and complex organ. Ancient people were often fascinated with the heart which was imagined to be an organ of endless territories and a place where gold could be found. What is mined in the depths of our hearts and souls used to be known as inner gold. This natural endowment of inner gold is the "treasure hard to attain."

Another way to consider the process of living in truth is to be mining the gold hidden in the heart and soul. The sense of spiritual gold being hidden in the heart permeates all the great religions and spiritual paths. Like the ore found in the deep veins of the earth, the inner gold has always been considered rare and valuable. Uncovering this spiritual essence and core of inner worth can be seen as the alchemical process of transforming the lead or weight of one's life into a gold that can be released into the world. Of course, our lives have to crack open many times in order for the hidden gold of our souls to be revealed. Then, in the strange alchemy of the soul, the value of the inner gold increases rather than diminishes from being freely given or being used in the service of the greater good of humanity.

At this time, when the divisions between people become greater and the cracks in the world keep getting bigger, I find myself thinking about a creative practice found in the ancient artistry of Japanese culture. The practice arises from the idea of *kintsukuroi*, or the "golden repair" of something treasured or important that has become cracked or broken. When applied to the repair of ancient and valuable pieces of pottery, the practice becomes *kintsugi*, or "golden joinery." The key to this imaginative art appears when the glue used to fill the cracks and join the broken pieces becomes blended with actual gold. After the repairs have been made, the broken vessel becomes more valuable than ever.

Metaphorically, *kintsugi* suggests that something may become more beautiful and more valuable after being broken if it becomes repaired with the gold of truth and imagination. Such a golden repair does not cover up the cracks in the vessel, nor does it deny the fact that something precious has been severely damaged. Rather, the painful splits and broken places become enduring evidence of a kind of gold that not only repairs, but also illuminates where the vessels of life have been harmed. In that sense, the process of repairing also becomes a way remembering how easily the most valuable things in life can be broken.

Like any genuine process of healing and making whole again, we must first acknowledge and study the exact faults and divisions that damage the vessels of our lives. If we could admit more readily to the tragic injuries that divide one group from another, we could replace the bloody damages with golden lines that serve to remind us of the fragility of life as well as the possibilities of repairing shattered dreams and redeeming broken lives.

In connection with the idea of living in truth, a golden repair of the world suggests redemptive practices through which the damages of history and the tragic mistakes we make with the fragile vessels of nature, culture, and individual lives might be repaired. Rather than shameful distortions to be disguised or hidden, the wounds we suffer and the healing of those wounds become a revelation of the hidden gold in the human soul. Beauty appears exactly where the wounds and faults existed as the golden scars add to the living story and to the enduring character of human life and living story of creation ongoing.

The practice of golden repair can be brought to bear wherever old wounds divide people; and in the many places where the increasing tragedies of violence and suicide leave people broken in spirit and at odds with the underlying beauty of life. Golden repair is needed in all the communities where tragedy has torn people apart, in all the places where trust has been shattered, where justice has been denied, where the earth has been ripped open and blindly exploited, where the healing presence of great forests have been turned into broad, unholy scars.

The wounds to the heart of humanity are too extensive and grievous for any single belief or ideology to heal. Just as each person has some golden qualities and a unique sense of being to bring to the world, each has the capacity to do some golden repair. Because the troubles of the world have grown so great and encompass most elements of both culture and nature, each person can find a wound, a division, or a crack nearby that can be turned into a golden seam. As the collective sense of unity in the common world collapses all around us, the uniqueness within individuals becomes an essential source of unifying imagination.

In mythical terms, it is not just a shift in politics that is needed; not only improvements in social justice, but also a reimagining of the whole design that can help weave culture back into balance with nature. Amidst all the confusion and chaos, all the false rhetoric and nihilistic ideas, our primary human task is to become the bearers of what genuine meaning and beauty we can envision and help reveal. When the problems of life become overwhelming and the tasks seem impossible, when everything seems hopeless and people feel helpless, we are being called to awaken to the wisdom of the underlying soul.

Either we awaken to the wisdom and resources of the soul, or we unwittingly contribute to the depreciation and dissolution of the world. Sometimes, the only safety in this world is found in taking the right risks. When the entire world seems to be at risk, safety may only come where we risk living in truth and following the call of our souls for the benefit of everyone. When the common institutions collapse and the usual cultural containers break, amidst all the conflicts and divisions plaguing the world, our role is to recover the true spirit for living and help reveal the underlying wholeness of life. If we envision the globe of the earth as a living, sacred vessel that needs artful repairs, we can imagine more ways of helping it heal. In the process, we may unburden our hearts and find our own Feather of Truth.

ACKNOWLEDGEMENTS

I want to express heartfelt gratitude to Coren Lindfield and Laura Rollins for much time and care spent shaping and crafting the book, to Kathleen Kelley for inspiration and attention to the heart of the book and to Molly Woolbright for editing in such a timely manner.

ABOUT MOSAIC

Mosaic Multicultural Foundation is a 501(c)3 nonprofit organization that has initiated innovative projects and unifying events that support and educate at-risk youth, refugees, combat veterans, and communities in need. Mosaic creates community through events involving artists, activists, community builders, healers, and spiritual teachers working in inspired ways to develop cross-cultural alliances, mentoring relationships, and forms of community healing.

Mosaic seeks to inspire awareness through community activities and creative ceremonies that reconnect people to meaningful traditions and the sacred ecology of place, while offering opportunities for personal growth, spiritual awakening, and leadership development. Mosaic publishes and produces the work of renowned storyteller and mythologist Michael Meade through an extensive collection of books, audio, essays and podcasts, as well as producing a full calendar of national and international community events.

Mosaic's projects include mentoring youth and awakening the wisdom of elders, finding common ground between those in opposition, shaping community events that unite people of various cultural and spiritual backgrounds, and encouraging greater understanding between people with diverse and divergent backgrounds and experiences. We address contemporary issues by combining traditional ideas and practices with fresh insights to reveal where new cultural forms can be conceived and developed.

GreenFire Press and **Mosaic Audio** are imprints of Mosaic Multicultural Foundation that serve to foster cultural literacy, mythic education, and multicultural community development. Proceeds from sales of books and recordings directly benefit Mosaic's work.

Books by Michael Meade

The Genius Myth
Fate and Destiny: The Two Agreements of Life
The World Behind the World: Living at the Ends of Time
Why the World Doesn't End
The Water of Life: Initiation and the Tempering of the Soul

Mosaic Audio Recordings by Michael Meade

A Song is a Road
Alchemy of Fire: Libido and the Divine Spark
Branches of Mentoring
The Ends of Time, the Roots of Eternity
Entering Mythic Territory: Healing and the Bestowing Self
The Eye of the Pupil, the Heart of the Disciple
Fate and Destiny: The Two Agreements in Life
Finding Genius in Your Life
The Great Dance: Finding One's Way in Troubled Times
Holding the Thread of Life: A Human Response to the Unraveling of the World
Inner Wisdom: The Eternal Youth and the Wise Old Sage
The Light Inside Dark Times
Initiation and the Soul: The Sacred and the Profane
Poetics of Peace: Peace and the Salt of the Earth
Poetics of Peace: Vital Voices in Troubled Times, with Alice Walker,
Luis Rodriguez, Jack Kornfield, Orland Bishop
The Soul of Change

Podcasts by Michael Meade

Living Myth, a free weekly podcast
Living Myth Premium, a membership-based podcast

Books edited by Michael Meade

Crossroads: The Quest For Contemporary Rites of Passage, edited by Louise
Carus Mahdi, Nancy Geyer Christopher, and Michael Meade
The Rag and Bone Shop of the Heart: A Poetry Anthology, edited by Robert
Bly, James Hillman, and Michael Meade

All books, audio and podcasts are available at mosaicvoices.org

GreenFire Press

An Imprint of Mosaic Multicultural Foundation

*All purchases support Mosaic's Genius-Based Mentoring,
Community Healing Events and Living Myth Project.*

P.O. Box 847, Vashon, WA 98070
(206) 935-3665
www.mosaicvoices.org ~ info@mosaicvoices.org